£ 6.95
£ 2.50
51

THE INTERPRETATION OF HOLY SCRIPTURE

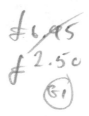
KT-514-508

220.6
D923i

THE INTERPRETATION of HOLY SCRIPTURE

WALTER M. DUNNETT

16076

THOMAS NELSON PUBLISHERS
Nashville • Camden • New York

Copyright © 1984 by Walter M. Dunnett

All rights reserved. Written permission must be secured from the publisher to use or reproduce any part of this book, except for brief quotations in critical reviews or articles.

Published in Nashville, Tennessee by Thomas Nelson, Inc., Publishers and distributed in Canada by Lawson Falle, Ltd., Cambridge, Ontario.

Printed in the United States of America.

Unless otherwise noted, the Bible version used in this publication is the Revised Standard Version of the Bible, copyrighted 1946, 1952, © 1971, 1973. Scripture quotations noted NEB, NIV, NASB, KJV, and TEV are from: *The New English Bible.* © The Delegates of the Oxford University Press and the Syndics of the Cambridge University Press 1961, 1970. Reprinted by permission; The Holy Bible: New International Version. Copyright © 1978 by the New York International Bible Society. Used by permission of Zondervan Bible Publishers; the New American Standard Bible, © the Lockman Foundation 1960, 1962, 1963, 1968, 1971, 1972, 1973, 1975, 1977, and are used by permission; the GOOD NEWS BIBLE: Copyright © American Bible Society 1966, 1971, 1976. Used by permission.

Library of Congress Cataloging in Publication Data

Dunnett, Walter M.
  The interpretation of Holy Scripture.

  Bibliography: pp. 201–210
  1. Bible—Hermeneutics. I. Title.
BS476.D82   1984   220.6'01   84-20557
ISBN 0-8407-5923-1

DEDICATED TO

Dolores

She is a person of
Integrity
and
She has stood
beside me

(GENESIS 2:18)

CONTENTS

ACKNOWLEDGMENTS

THE BASIC RESEARCH and first draft of this work was done at Tyndale House and the Cambridge University Library in England. Thanks go to the Warden of Tyndale House, Murray J. Harris, and its Librarian, Craig Broyles, for help in locating materials and for sundry kindnesses during my sabbatical term. Professor E. Earle Ellis of New Brunswick Theological Seminary graciously contributed his time and gave helpful suggestions. For these I thank him heartily. Drs. Donald and Beverly Hagner of Pasadena, California provided a number of stimulating insights and frequent encouragements over numerous cups of tea. Thanks also go to Dr. Grant Osborne of Trinity Evangelical Divinity School. My wife, Dolores, and I shared the task of typing and retyping the manuscript, and I deeply appreciate her willingness to assume this extra work load. Finally, a word of appreciation is due Larry Stone and Ronald Pitkin of Thomas Nelson, Publishers, for counsel and motivation in the production of this work and to Paul Franklyn for his editorial expertise, giving the work an improved appearance.

INTRODUCTION

THE IMPETUS FOR this book came from a growing interest in certain issues involved in reading and teaching the Bible to college-age students and to church classes devoted to Bible study. Anyone engaged in such instruction often raises these questions: What does this text mean? How should one go about discovering its meaning? What is its significance for today? How can I apply this teaching to my own life?

Commonly this procedure of interpretation is called hermeneutics, a term basically meaning "the science and art of interpretation." It is a science because it contains certain ingredients awaiting examination—a text to be read, rules of grammar to be applied, and a basic meaning of language to be discovered; it is an art because it calls for effort to be expended in a creative, skillful manner to obtain a desired result. As to the former, one must avoid a purely mechanical approach in handling the language of the Bible; as to the latter, one must guard against an arbitrary or subjective approach.

Today we smile at H. Wheeler Robinson's statement (written in 1943) about hermeneutics as "a rather neglected branch of Biblical study at the present time."[1] Such neglect is no more since hermeneutics has been an area of keen interest among students of the Bible for over thirty years. In 1980 the editor of *Themelios* referred to the problem of hermeneutics and the related issue of contextualization as "a subject that is not going to go away.... the questions that are raised by the study of these two problems will be with us well into the next decade."[2]

In view of the current interest and concern, this book

intends to address a number of issues related to the whole task of interpreting the Bible. These issues are diverse, yet all contribute to more complete understanding and facilitate the expression or communication of biblical teaching. First, there are methodological issues; second, there are ideological issues; third, there are historical issues; and, finally, there are principles for doing interpretation and making application of the text of Scripture.

Chapter one will deal with certain issues in methodology—how we approach the transfer of meaning from one language to another; that is, the problem of translating the Bible from Hebrew and Greek to a modern language such as English or French. In addition to questions about the meaning of a text, we must also ask about the significance of the text for those to whom it is addressed. There is also the related question about the sense of the text—whether one is to interpret in a literal or a nonliteral sense.

Chapter two tackles one of the thorniest, yet one of the most important, ideological issues of the day; namely, the idea of the authority of the Bible. If we grant that the Bible is an authority for many people, we must wrestle with the questions of why and how? A number of answers have been given but one thing is clear. If the Bible is to be truly authoritative, it must be so both cognitively and functionally. That is to say, in the realm of knowledge and in the realm of action it must be "the Word of God." It is important to affirm what it is and what it does.

Chapter three will discuss another ideological issue; namely, the question of the meaning of revelation and inspiration. If we regard revelation as necessary, then we should ask: How has God made himself known? What are the forms of revelation? Is revelation characterized by acts of God or by his speech? Then in whatever forms revelation has occurred, how has it been transmitted? And what assurance have we of its trustworthiness? These questions will lead us to discuss the idea of inspiration, a term occurring once in the Bible that refers to a "divine breathing" of the message. For some, inspiration is crucial as a "guarantee" of the authenticity of the message. For others, it amounts to an effect on the writers apart from any necessary effect on what was written. The discussion of these issues continues as a lively debate today.

Chapters four to six will attempt to give some historical perspective and insight into the ways in which the Bible has been interpreted throughout the history of the Christian church. Chapter four is a somewhat detailed study of the use of the Old Testament in the New; chapter five looks at the centuries from the first to nineteenth; chapter six at the twentieth century. Discovering how the Bible has been interpreted before our time can be both instructive and humbling. We shall see the main trends in interpretation and the principles employed, some of which will be eye openers for today's student of Scripture. One may soon be asking how people of equally devout spirit could arrive at such different interpretations of the same texts. (Of course, we will be pleased to observe that such different people have arrived at basic areas of agreement.)

In the history of Christian interpretation, the New Testament stands as the earliest example of dealing with the meaning and significance of the Old Testament. How did Jesus and the early disciples understand "their Bible"? Are we able to follow their example? Will we arrive at the same conclusions? As "the foundational principle of exegesis," modern readers must try to enter into their world, to wear their shoes, and share the same perceptions, thoughts and feelings as did our first century predecessors.[3]

The remaining parts of the book deal with interpretation directly. Chapters seven to ten discuss principles of exegesis, and chapter eleven deals with models of exegesis. Chapter seven discusses the basic aspects of language; namely, the text of Scripture, the basic meaning and history of the use of words, grammar and syntax (how words relate to each other in a basic unit such as the sentence), and the local context of any particular unit of thought. Chapter eight deals with the literary forms occurring in the Bible, whether prose, poetry, narrative, or didactic (teaching) materials, as well as wisdom literature and apocalyptic writings. Included also are a variety of figures of speech, whether metaphor and simile, or proverb and parable. Fifteen or more examples of these are included, using many illustrations from the biblical text. In chapter nine the historical and cultural context of the Bible will be discussed by trying to show both the framework for the writings and the various historical and cultural aspects included in the writings. We will explain that the Babylonian attack upon Jerusalem and its temple is the historical context of the book of Jeremiah, or we could study the burial of Jesus. In both cases the reader attempts to apprehend the setting understood by the writers or readers of biblical times. Chapter ten attempts to discern the theological context of the writings of the Bible. What does the text teach about God, his relations to the created world, and human life? Are there theological themes to be found, such as grace, mercy, redemption, hope or judgment? Presumably, these theological issues will enable the transfer of an ancient message into the modern age.

Finally a series of exegetical models will be presented in chapter eleven. These represent various types of literature within the Bible—an Old Testament narrative, a prophetic passage, a miracle story in the New Testament, a Gospel narrative, a parable, and a theological passage in a New Testament epistle. The approach in each of these is a step-by-step illustration of how one might do exegetical and theological study together with implicit or explicit application to the reader.

THE INTERPRETATION
OF HOLY SCRIPTURE

CHAPTER ONE

Fundamental Issues

ONE OF THE most famous dialogues in literature was that between Alice and Humpty Dumpty. It concerned the meaning of words.

> H.D.: "There's glory for you!"
> A.: "But I don't know what you mean by 'glory'."
> H.D.: "I mean, 'There's a nice knock-down argument for you'."
> A.: "But—'glory' doesn't mean 'a nice knock-down argument'."
> H.D.: "When I use a word," Humpty Dumpty said, in rather a scornful tone, "it means just what I choose it to mean—neither more nor less."
> A.: "The question is," said Alice, "whether you can *make* words mean so many different things."
> H.D.: "The question is" said Humpty Dumpty, "which is to be master—that's all."

The heart of the matter is what we mean by what we say and how well those who hear (or read) understand the message we are trying to communicate.

Emphasis on the text

When one reads the Bible an additional factor is added to the problem of understanding. The Bible is an ancient book. Instead of asking in this case, "What *does* it mean?" we first must ask, "What *did* it mean?" Thus readers of the Bible, and all who would explain it to others, are faced with the double problem of the "then" and the "now."

Consider an example of this twofold process in the New Testament: (1) Acts 8:32–35; (2) 1 Pet. 2:21–23.

Now the passage of the scripture which he was reading was this:

> "As a sheep led to the slaughter
> or a lamb before its shearer is dumb,
> so he opens not his mouth.
> In his humiliation justice was denied him.
> Who can describe his generation?
> For his life is taken up from the earth."

And the eunuch said to Philip, "About whom, pray, does the prophet say this, about himself or about someone else?" Then Philip opened his mouth, and beginning with this scripture he told him the good news of Jesus.

For to this you have been called, because Christ also suffered for you, leaving you an example, that you should follow in his steps. He committed no sin; no guile was found on his lips. When he was reviled, he did not revile in return; when he suffered, he did not threaten; but he trusted to him who judges justly.

In both these passages the author is explaining the text of Isa. 53:7, particularly the clause, "So he did not open his mouth." The first example is a story of a man who read this passage, then asked the evangelist Philip, "Concerning whom did the prophet (Isaiah) say this? Was it about himself or about another person?" In response Philip identifies the passage as a prophecy about Jesus—Christ is identified as the one who suffered without opening his mouth.

In the second example the apostle Peter appeals to the same text, Isa. 53:7, assuming it to be spoken about Jesus. He now applies it to the life-situation of his "servant" readers (see v. 18). When Christ suffered, says Peter, he did not reply in kind nor threaten his enemies. That stands as an example for you; you should respond as your Master did (see also 1 Pet. 3:9, where the teaching is applied to the entire audience).

This kind of approach, reading the Bible in terms of what it *meant* and what it *means*, has been rather typical for many years. Rules of interpretation have been formulated to help Bible students in their understanding. In the eighteenth century, J. A. Ernesti wrote that hermeneutics "consists in general principles of interpretation," which are to be followed by "the application of those general principles to the interpretation of particular passages."[1]

What was the point of "interpretation"? According to Ernesti, it was "the art of teaching the real sentiment contained in any form of words" so that a reader could derive from the words the same idea that the writer intended to convey. And what did this imply about language? It said that "the literal sense" (or the primitive meaning) of words is "the sense in which the word is, or was ordinarily used at the time of writing." That sense is what we must look for. In other words, what did Moses, David, Matthew, or Paul mean to say to the original audience that they addressed?

Because many words change their meanings over a period of years, this original sense may or may not be known to the hearer or reader. Readers of English today may or may not know, for example, that "sincere" originally meant "without wax"; or that "precise" meant "cut off at the end"; or that "wrong" meant "twisted."[2] This awareness will caution us against reading back more recent meanings into the biblical text. For example, Paul described the gospel or the "power" of God (Rom. 1:16). The Greek word for "power" here is *dynamis*. It meant force, might, strength, or ability. From this word we get our English term "dynamite," referring to a substance containing the explosive nitroglycerin. Occasionally one hears the expression, "The gospel is God's dynamite." But the sense here is quite different from the earlier one, as it reads back a physical concept into a conceptual one. It is not a safe procedure to describe earlier concepts in terms of later meanings ascribed to the same set of symbols (words).

What we must do, therefore, is to search first of all for the meaning indicated by the Bible writer; that meaning indicated by the words that are used in the text. For many in earlier times, and today, a departure from this single literal sense was considered to be an error in interpreting language.

This view actually has a long history and has produced any number of guidelines for interpretation; for example, (1) begin with the ordinary meaning of the language, (2) identify the type of language being used (whether prose or poetry, literal or figurative), and (3) seek a single meaning for what the author has said.[3] In the same vein, F. D. E. Schleiermacher drew up two principles of interpretation which insisted on (1) attention to the language common to the author and his original public, and (2) the importance of the context in determining the meaning of any word in a particular passage.[4]

Emphasis on the reader

Yet in recent times, the basic question asked by many interpreters is not "what did/does this text mean?" but "In what way, or to whom, is it meaningful?" Thus, a move has been made from "what?" to "how?" signalling a shift to the art of interpretation.[5] This has resulted in a greater emphasis on the means of understanding a text and how understanding may be consciously initiated in each individual case. Schleiermacher showed how ideas were represented by words; that is, how universal concepts were seen in particular symbols.[6]

What does this newer approach mean for the interpreter? Basically, each person must be aware of one's own subjectivity— one's own presuppositions, cultural orientation, and psychological capabilities. This awareness is intended to initiate genuine understanding of the text. We must be aware of the distance between ourselves and the biblical writers. We need to be aware that the ancient world view and mindset are different in many respects. Only as we do so can we achieve success in understanding the text.

Suppose we illustrate the tension between these two approaches by considering the work of the Bible translator whose task is to bring an ancient text into a modern setting. The United Bible Societies employ a principle called "dynamic equivalence" that directs the translator to produce for the reader or hearer in the receptor language (the language of the one receiving the message) the same reaction to the message that the original writer tried to produce for his readers or hearers. Now the focus of attention has shifted from the form of the message ("this is what the text actually said in the original language") to the response of the receptor ("this is what it means to the hearer or reader"). Thus the question for the translator is not simply, "Is this a correct translation?" but, "For whom?"[7]

Further, the "dynamic equivalence" approach asserts that as each language has its own genius such genius must be respected in doing translation. Unless the *form* of the message is an essential element of the communication, it can be changed to communicate *content*. This may be illustrated by looking at the phrase "white as snow" since the word "snow" is not crucial to the message; that is, the idea of whiteness could be communicated apart from comparison with snow. Or again, in attempting to tell Eskimos that "the Lord is my shepherd," what might be an acceptable equivalent in that culture for the concept of "sheep"? Finally the expression "lively oracles" (Acts 7:38 KJV) is changed to "living utterances" (NEB) or "living messages" (TEV).

Nida and Taber have made some basic observations on the nature of the biblical languages:[8]

(1) They have the same limitations as any human language. For example, they contain ambiguities or they employ special uses of common words, etc. What does "the love of God" mean (1 John 2:5)? Is it "love for God" (RSV, TEV) or is it "divine love" (NEB)? Also such everyday terms in the ancient

world as redeem, justify, or save are often used in special senses in the Bible.

(2) The biblical writers wrote to be understood. They intended one meaning in what they wrote. Thus our attempts at translating the content should be marked by that same aim of clarity and contemporaneity.

(3) The translator must respect the writer's intent, thus making every effort to reproduce the meaning understood by the writer.

Theological and linguistic criticism of this "dynamic equivalence" approach has come from a number of quarters. This school of thought rejects the orthodox doctrine of Christ by making him and his words subject to all first century limitations. It also denies that the Bible reveals absolute truth transcending the time in which it was written. While divine revelation aims to restore divine-human communication, it is not itself part of the communication event. Again, it confuses people present and people addressed by the Word of God, thus limiting God's message to ancient times. This vitiates the idea of timeless or universal truths. Further, it does not account for the creation of man in God's image or the unity of the race in Adam. The basic reality of human life is not the great cultural differences but "the one history of God's dealings with the one human race in Adam," that is, that God had made man so that he might hear the divine message (compare 1 Cor. 2:6–16; Acts 17:24–28). The message was not for the original hearers alone (1 Pet. 1:11–12; Rom. 15:4).[9]

The basic theological issue here, with important consequences for linguistics, is the reality of the unity of the human race in guilt before and punishment by God (see Rom. 1:18–32). A call for conversion is heard in the biblical revelation, and a response to the call will enable us to acknowledge God and to understand his revelation. In Scripture, it is basically sin, not a difference in the cultures of the receptors, that is the root of the problem.

Our task, then, is to render the message, not simply to

transmit it in a way that gives the needs of the receptor priority over the original form of the message. Notice the following illustrations of the problem: Rev. 5:5: "the Root of David" (KJV); "the great descendant of David" (TEV). The change from "Root" to "great descendant" definitely shifts the message away from the idea of the pre-existence of Christ and places the emphasis on his humanity rather than his deity (compare John 8:56–58). Ps. 110:4: "after the order of Melchizedek" (RSV); "in the line of succession to Melchizedek" (TEV, 1976). The text of this psalm speaks of a class of priests living forever (compare Heb. 7:3). Thus one can hardly speak of a succession of priests.

The literary form of an author's sentence ought to be respected in the receptor language as far as possible. Otherwise, more interpretation than necessary—even a change—may be added to the rendering. A reliable translation should exhibit faithfulness to form, clarity of expression, completeness, loyalty to the text, a spiritual insight and sensitivity, authoritativeness, and ecclesiastical usage.[10]

Let us try to grasp the essence of each of these approaches to interpreting the Bible and retain the strengths that are there. On the one hand, if we emphasize the form of the message (retaining the literal meaning of the text), we are attempting to remain true to the message as originally given. We want to know what Jeremiah "actually wrote" and what he "actually meant." We want to hear his, "Thus says the Lord." This is an important viewpoint, for it insists that the words of the Bible are God's words, "the absolute revelation from heaven," and not "merely a part of a culturally confined communication event."[11]

On the other hand, the desire to communicate the Word of God to each generation and each culture is important because the Bible was not given simply for ancient times. Its message needs to be transmitted in meaningful language. This mediating approach is taken by the Reformer Martin Luther. For Luther, "the appropriate interpretation of a text lay neither in the recovery of the unique literal sense nor in the unfolding of multi-level meanings, but in the discovery of the legitimate meaning, based on grammatical and historical analysis, informed by theological reflection, and applied to one's own life and the church of the present." Luther was unwilling to draw a sharp distinction between "what the text meant" and "what it means."[12]

What, then, of the tension between these two basic approaches to rendering the meaning of the biblical text? Is a grammatical, historical approach or the road of dynamic equivalence to be sought? If one follows the former, so the charge is levelled, one retains the distance between writer and reader. The translation/interpretation may be faithful to the text but possibly unintelligible to the reader. On the other hand, the latter attempts to reduce the historical, linguistic gap, thus making the text meaningful, yet the danger is the "modernizing" of the text which may result in a loss of the original sense intended by the writer.

Returning to some familiar terms, we may say that this represents a tension between interpretation and application. In the whole process of recovering the meaning of Scripture, both elements need to be retained. They represent "two sides of a coin," and to lose sight of either will result in loss to the reader.

The purpose of this book as it develops is to attempt this sort of resolution. We shall enter into the quest along with others by looking at Scripture itself to gain perspective and, hopefully, principles of interpretation; by seeing what biblical scholars through the years have attempted to do; by discussing the current scene in the quest for sound interpretation; and by suggesting approaches, principles, and examples of exegesis for biblical texts.

Variety and continuity

Several other issues relating to the subject of interpretation will be considered briefly here and are discussed more fully in the chapters which follow.

First, there is the issue of whether a single or multiple meanings are to be found in any Bible text. Did the writer have just one subject or theme in mind? Or is a text open to more than one? The answer to the question is dependent on one's view of the nature of language as well as one's view of the authorship of the Bible. As to the former, any word or set of words is theoretically open to several meanings. Take as an example the word "orange." Do I have in mind a piece of fruit, a flavor, or a round object? Consciously I may think of the fruit, yet the flavor could well be a closely associated idea. As to the latter point, is the Bible a divine book (that is, God's word) as well as a human book, (that is, man's word)? If both these authorships are accepted it should be asked if there might be a meaning beyond that which the human author had in mind? Take as an example the statement, "out of Egypt I called my son" (Hos. 11:1). By reading this entire passage carefully one is quite certain that the prophet had referred to God calling the Israelites out of slavery in Egypt, the event we call the Exodus. Can the passage go beyond that? Evidently so according to Matt. 2:15, where the return of Joseph and Mary and Jesus to Nazareth (2:23) was regarded as a "fulfillment" of Hosea's prophecy. Yet, we may ask, did Hosea have that in mind?

This introduces a second, larger issue; namely, the relation of the Old Testament and the New Testament. Is there a basic continuity or a discontinuity between the testaments? Is the life and worship of the early Church a continuation of, or a deviation from, the life and worship of the Hebrew people in the history of Israel? For the Christian reader at least two answers are possible. One is that the "full word of God" has come in Christ and that the Old Testament serves basically as a background or a preparation of some kind. Such readers tend to think mainly in terms of discontinuity. Some have virtually ruled out the Old Testament to one degree or another for Christians—that is, in a dispensational theology or by such noted figures as Marcion (second century A.D.) or R. Bultmann.

A second answer is that the revelation of God is basically continuous—the Old Testament was the first stage while the New Testament was the culmination. Such a view is reflected in the opening words of the epistle to the Hebrews: "In many and various ways God spoke of old to our fathers by the prophets; but in these last days he has spoken to us by a Son" (Heb. 1:1–2). Other indications would be the use of the same promises in both testaments (see Jer. 31:31–34 and Heb. 8:8–12) or the use of what is called typology (an event, person, or object in the Old foreshadows something in the New; see John 3:14–15; Heb. 7:1–3).

Third, another issue is that of the relation of faith and history and the nature of each. What is history? Is it the brute facts? Is it what people said or wrote? Is it physical events occurring at specific locations? We may assert that Columbus discovered America in 1492. That event certainly involved ships and people and weather conditions. No doubt certain words were spoken and possibly written. Much of this data is lost to us forever, yet the arrival of Columbus constitutes a historical event. That event has been affirmed by certain kinds of evidences—documents, names of ships and people, and so on. However, one reading the history of that event must evaluate the evidence, assess its significance, and grasp the reasons or causes for the event.

Biblical history contains records of events such as the accession and reign of King David, the Babylonian captivity, or the travels of the apostle Paul. We may center on very specific incidents such as the crucifixion of Christ or the Exodus under Moses. What is the nature of this "history"? And what is its significance? In the Bible the first element in any event was the presence and activity of God. The purpose of God is what gives meaning to events. Consider Paul's statement of the death of Christ (1 Cor. 15:3): (1) Christ died; (2) for our sins; (3) in accordance with the Scriptures. The first statement describes a "historical" event; the second gives a theological interpretation of it; while the third calls it a fulfillment of prophecy. Statements (2) and (3) are "faith" statements; they are not based on simple observation. At this point the element of divine revelation is important. God made known to the biblical writer the significance of an event. That is why we encounter the issue of biblical authority.

CHAPTER TWO

The Authority of the Bible

AUTHORITY IS THAT which compels attention, assent, or obedience. The concept when applied to the Bible is complex, for it resolves itself into two basic questions, each of which has received various answers. The two questions are: (1) *Why* is the Bible authoritative and (2), assuming a positive attitude toward the idea, *how* is the Bible authoritative?

Why is the Bible authoritative?

Generally, the answer to this question is that, in some sense, "the Bible is the Word of God." Such a response certainly evokes the idea of authority. If the Bible is so regarded, it shares in the same qualities that God possesses (such as truth and righteousness) and reveals God's will, thus being "the instrument of rule over our lives."[1]

Further, from a Lutheran perspective, the basis for the authority of the Bible is "its relation to the revelation of the living God," and God's revelation of himself is the dominating theme of the Bible.[2] This basic idea is found also in R. Bultmann,[3] radical as he has seemed to many. The Bible does not approach us like any other book or religious voice. From the start it claims to be God's Word. The church proclaims, "God speaks to you here!" That is an authoritative summons to which we must listen.

Once more, "the question of the authority of Scripture is the question of the nature of the revelation and the nature of the God who is revealed and the relation of that revelation

13

and that God to the life of the church and to the life of the world."[4] Thus it is primary to discover what Scripture says concerning itself and the God revealed there.

These samplings, from a variety of sources, give an impression as to the importance of the concept of authority based on divine revelation. If the Bible in any sense is "God's Word" it is an authoritative word.

Yet such a position has raised some questions. First, does such an idea focus the question wrongly? Do we attribute authority to a book? Should not the Bible's own witness to Christ as "the Word of God" (John 1:1) be heard? Was not the authority of Jesus Christ the actual authority for the New Testament Church? It appears Christ himself distinguished between the written Word and its testimony to him, and left little question where true life resided (see John 5:39f. NIV): "you diligently study the Scriptures because you think that by them you possess eternal life. These are the Scriptures that testify about me, yet you refuse to come to me to have life"). In a related manner C. K. Barrett notes that the authority of Scripture resides in "the effectiveness with which it points to the central event...in the clarity of the witness they [the Gospels] bear to Jesus Christ."[5]

In these statements we see a move toward a *functional* view of the authority of the Bible. This popular view may be stated, for the moment, in pragmatic terms: the Bible possesses authority "because it works." Some who hold this functional view will emphasize "the truth of the gospel"—or, its witness to the life, death, and resurrection of Jesus Christ—as the essential core of Scripture. The Bible contains the words and acts of God bringing salvation. It is an effective message.[6]

In a recent statement the American evangelical theologian, C. F. H. Henry, criticizes the functional view of biblical authority since it deprives the Bible of any fixed intellectual content. Thus it is "inspiring" rather than an "inspired" text. It does away with its propositional authority and normativity.[7]

Henry's position recognizes some basic theological aspects of Scripture; namely, the twin (or often related) themes of revelation and inspiration. This affirms that God had disclosed himself, not in acts alone but in speech, and that this revelatory activity has been faithfully recorded by the inspiration of the Holy Spirit (based on various biblical affirmations, such as 2 Pet. 1:19–21 or 1 Pet. 1:10–11).

One can certainly discover many indications of the "inspired words" in Scripture.[8] In the Old Testament, the prophets frequently claim "the word of the Lord came to me" (Jer. 1:4) and that God put his words in their mouths (Jer. 1:9). They speak and write with a sense of divine authority, "Thus says the Lord." So also in the New Testament; "not as the word of men, but as it actually is, the word of God, which is at work in you who believe" (1 Thess. 2:13 NIV). This claim to the authoritative speech of the prophet or apostle was then transferred to the written word; that is, 2 Tim. 3:16 referring to the "Scripture" (the sacred writings, v. 15); or Rev. 22:18–19 referring to "the words of the prophecy of this book" and ultimately to the canon of Scripture.

The importance of a trustworthy Bible is widely recognized, especially when interpreting the text. One must take seriously the Bible's witness to itself, and this would appear to involve the entire Bible.[9] Without getting mired in a continual defense of Scripture or always debating about minor points, we need to listen to the Bible's own claims to authority.

A second question linked to the concept of authority, based on the Bible's self-attestation as "God's Word," is that of the relation of the divine and human elements in Scripture. The central thesis of a recent book is, *the Bible is the Word of God given in the words of men in history.*[10] This raises a major problem. How, at the same time, can the words of men be the eternal word of God?

For the last two hundred years, scholars have emphasized the importance of interpreting the Bible from a historical point of view. It was written within human history and by human writers. The humanity of the writers was respected. They were not simply mechanical secretaries. The process of writing was not a kind of dictation in which they were essentially passive. There is an interplay in the Bible between "the Word of God to man" and "the Word of Israel, the Word of the church to God" (as a human response).[11]

We are faced here with the relation between history and theology, between faith and historical criticism. The relativity of ancient history, its distance and difference from our modern situation causes us to ask how the two can be related. Because all historical writing involves interpretation, we ask about the respective assumptions and grounds for interpretation held both by the writers of the Bible and the modern interpreters. To put it in a modern idiom, are we on the same "wave length"?

Various attempts are made by biblical scholars to respond to this set of problems.[12] One attempt sees history in a unilinear sense—the so-called tabernacling presence—as God is present with his people throughout their history. Not all portions of the Bible, however, were characterized by this model.

A second approach is that of typology. The Old Testament in its central events, persons, and key words is a foreshadowing and anticipation of the New Testament. Hence a basic continuity is established within the biblical record as a whole. Yet a weakness of this approach is a tendency to diminish the unique historical revelation of the Old Testament.

Third, others regard the biblical theology of the Old Testament as "a confessional recital of the redemptive acts of God" (a phrase used by G. E. Wright). By repetition the message is made contemporary; that is, later generations try to "relive" the historical experiences of their ancestors. This becomes a way for a later interpreter and the biblical speaker/ writer to be brought closer together in the present. A danger here is the possible distortion of the original historical character of the message in attempting to "modernize" it.

A fourth attempt is centered in the Christological character of the Bible—the Old Testament anticipated and the New Testament fulfilled the messianic hope. Without a knowledge of Israel's faith, the message about Christ is greatly impoverished. Without a realization of the fulfillment in the life and ministry of Christ in the New Testament, the Old Testament is left without its full impact. A key problem here is the danger of reading too much into the texts of the Old Testament, thereby "forcing" a meaning foreign to the message.

In all these attempts—and others that might be considered— one message comes through clearly. We need to be both interpreters and hearers. We must approach the text as fully aware as we can, and we must also listen to the message of the text. We must regard the Bible as a truly historical document—with whatever distance from us and strangeness to us that is involved—and yet see in history the reality of divine revelation.

This problem of revelation and history is emphasized at Isa. 55:8—"For my thoughts are not your thoughts, neither are your ways my ways, says the Lord." The revelation of God (his thoughts and his ways) comes in human forms (our thoughts and our ways). Three ways of looking at this paradox are suggested.[13]

First, one contemporary view states that revelation is dynamic instead of static. Rather than having a fixed content that may be analyzed, it is dynamic action that is apprehended personally (or existentially). Thus revelation comes in forms that are as the husk to the kernel. The forms tell us what God has done—his Word is powerful in its effects. Historical events convey the meaning of the Word of God. Yet there is a gap between fact and faith. Faith interprets the facts; the facts in themselves do not account for the faith. This may be seen by observing that many read the facts but fail to see in them a "faith perspective."

Second, we see two dissenting approaches to this paradox; namely, orthodoxy and liberalism. Though these two schools of thought differ in many respects, they agree in opposing this paradox because God has spoken in history and his revelation can be discerned therein. Revelation and inspiration are nearly equated. For orthodoxy the gap between fact and faith is bridged. The Bible is God's Word written. Faith answers the demands of facts, and the facts are certain, being assured by inspiration. For liberalism, the contents of the Bible are not regarded as revelation, per se. The message is to be empirically verified; what can be demonstrated as "true" should be accepted. Both the meaning of the facts and the ethical values of biblical teaching are subject to rational human verification.

There is no simple solution to the problem of the relation of the human and the divine in Scripture. History as the vehicle of God's self-revelation and the divine interpretation of the historical revelation belong together. There is a unity which G. E. Ladd has called the "revealing deed-word event" (see Exod. 4:28–31),[14] a phenomenon frequently seen in the books of the prophets in the Old Testament. Thus the Bible is "interpreted history—history understood as the vehicle of God's self-revelation and saving acts."

How is this history made contemporaneous? Again, there are several answers because one may approach the issue from several directions. One answer is to appeal to the work of the Holy Spirit in the church, a kind of "holy tradition," which brings the prophetic words of Scripture "to life," or "into life." This is seen in the New Testament with the contemporizing of Christ's experience of death in baptism (Rom. 6:3–4) or with a sharing in the resurrection and the sufferings of Christ (Phil. 3:10). An "evangelical criticism" is one making room for both historical and revelatory aspects of the Bible.[15]

Another answer is to discover a "common situation" that relates the ancient people with modern people. Though the Bible is an ancient book and many of its texts seem not to apply to our present life, within the church it "builds and enriches the faith" so that people may see their own situation with greater clarity and judge their actions more rightly.[16] We realize that human societies, though separated by time and geography, are not "closed" and that experiences common to people recur. Further, there is the sharing of "the people of God" through the ages. We share a common relation both on a horizontal and a vertical dimension.

A third approach is to reconsider the nature of the "history" contained in the Bible. This is a thorny issue, to say the least. Yet there may be need to recall that "history" in the biblical sense is more than "facts" or "events." D. Stacey has noted that a Hebrew account of reality embraces a composite structure; namely, (1) the purpose of God, (2) the happening, and (3) subsequent apprehension of the purpose through the happening.[17] These "true events" are "centres of power," and by remembering the past or by rehearsing it, we may experience "a formal re-living of the great event." This idea is based on the belief that what God did once he will do again.

Obviously much of the Bible is not written as historical narrative. There are psalms, proverbs, prophetic oracles, and epistles. We encounter both prose and poetry. We read of laws for the life of Israel and the commands of apostles directed to the churches of the first century. How do these materials apply to modern readers? Aside from what has been noted in the first observation above, we can add a fourth point here: The Bible, understood as fully as possible, was given to provide eternal principles for the lives of the people of God, not directly to solve every current problem. Once again, this will call for the Holy Spirit to bring the message of Scripture to "a living and active" state in the church. Not only do we need to practice exegesis of the text to discover what the original writer meant, but we need to exercise discernment in judging what is enduring and what is contingent. We study the past not simply to discover the old but the eternal. To be indebted to the past does not mean to be bound by it.[18]

How is the Bible authoritative?

In answer to this question we may build upon some of the responses to our first question. The Bible is authoritative because it is in some sense "the Word of God"; it is an authoritative summons calling for decision and obedience; it is the vehicle of salvation since it declares our need for, and points us to, Jesus Christ.

If we say that the Bible is authoritative because it is "the

Word of God," we must ask how it becomes the Word of God? It is or should be clear that we cannot simply equate the "words" of Scripture with "the Word" of God. Or, to put it in other terms, there is a profound difference between "the letter" of Scripture and "the-word-of-God-character" of Scripture.

This is illustrated, first, in some of the statements in the Gospels that describe Jesus' encounters with religious figures of his day. Notice the distinction he drew between the Scriptures read as "letter" and the Scriptures perceived truly as divine (Matt. 15:3–6; Mark 7:6–13); or his distinction between the "words" of the Old Testament and the divine witness to himself (John 5:38–39). The true "Word of God" is a mystery known only to believers, while to others this understanding has not been granted (Matt. 13:11). Further, it is possible to "read Moses" (that is, the Torah, "the Word of God") and yet to have a veil over one's heart (2 Cor. 3:15). Even Torah as a written record is not "the Word of God" to all who read.

What makes the difference? It is that "the letter kills, but the Spirit gives life" (2 Cor. 3:6). It is the "word hidden" and the "word revealed." The Word of God is not a static or abstract concept but living, dynamic, and spiritual.

> The distinctive feature . . . is that the concept of knowledge in the Old Testament is not determined by the idea that the reality of what is known is most purely grasped when personal elements are obliterated between the subject and object of knowledge, and knowledge is reduced to contemplation from without. On the contrary, the Old Testament both perceives and asserts the significance and claim of the knowing subject.[19]

Again, "this is the work of the Spirit and the Word, and is beyond that of the literary critic—unless it breaks through to them precisely in the exercise of their craft."[20]

Another factor relating to the "how" question is that of obedience to the authoritative Word of God. In the Bible a lack of knowledge of what God says is not primarily intellectual; rather it is volitional. It is a defect in the will rather than in the intellect. In one word, it is "disobedience" to the expressed will of God. When the Lord speaks about Israel "not knowing" or "not understanding" (Isa. 1:3), the problem is laid out by the use of such terms as "revolted," "act corruptly," "turn away from," and "rebellion" (vv. 2, 4, 5). To know whether or not Jesus' teachings are of God, one must be "willing to do His will" (John 7:17 NASB). The things which Jesus taught on one occasion were hidden by God from the "wise and intelligent" and revealed to "babes" (Luke 10:21). True understanding comes only through the revelation centered in and given by the Son (v. 22). This authority possessed by the Son, and revealing the Word of God to men, "cannot be understood except where there is a willingness and humility to bow before it as the authority of God himself."[21]

Thus the Scriptures possess authority to those who are willing to hear and obey. This is a powerful reminder of the reality of what the Bible calls "sin"—at root a rebellion against divine authority, an unwillingness to acknowledge and receive the wisdom of God. The natural man, Paul stated, is aware of what "the things of the Spirit of God" are, but he does not "welcome" them, nor does he "embrace the realities represented by the Bible's teachings" (1 Cor. 2:14).[22] What is needed here is the Spirit's work to bring a change in the heart of the interpreter. Through sin's deceitfulness we have come to trust in human wisdom instead of loving God with our whole heart.

A third aspect of the question is to notice the ways in which the Bible speaks to the human situation, once more coming with the voice of authority to those willing to hear it. This is not necessarily followed by obedience. We may (and often do) hear and understand, yet choose not to obey.

This word of authority and the ensuing response is often seen in the lives and speeches of prophets or apostles in the Bible. When Nathan pronounced judgment on David—"You are the man!"—through the parable about the two sheep-holders, David confessed, "I have sinned against the Lord" (2 Sam. 11:1–14). When Amos pronounced sentence upon the house of Israel, Amaziah the priest of Bethel, ordered him to flee away and not to prophesy in the royal residence of Jeroboam II (Amos 7:7–13). The same reaction may be observed after the speeches of John the Baptizer, of Jesus, and of his apostles (for example, "Paul, you are out of your mind! Your great learning is driving you mad. But Paul said, I am not out of my mind most excellent Festus, but I utter words of sober truth." Acts 26:24–25).

Can people today hear the authoritative Word of God? H. E. W. Turner has stated, "If contemporary man is to receive the forgiveness of God he must even today have sufficient receptivity or attunedness, adequate loyalty to the past in which God has been at work and enough humility to sit down before the facts and hear the word of the Lord as it comes to us through them."[23]

We need to allow the Scriptures to confront us, to question our prejudices, and to examine "the thoughts and intents of the heart." We need to search for or listen for a reply from the text. For some the key question from the text concerns the meaning and significance of our lives; the key answer is a positive affirmation that, indeed, "life is for something." There is purpose and opportunity before us. Yet these elements are defined in terms of the Risen One who is Lord of the Church.[24] It is his call, his promise, his direction for his church which is the directive for the present day.

William Countryman has identified three basic things which one might expect from any authority:[25] (1) a sense of identity and hope, (2) a set of norms for belief and behavior, and (3) some eternal checks to tell us how we stand in relation to hope and norms. This model can be illustrated from the relationships within a family or from the tasks of a national government. He asks whether the Bible fulfills these functions and whether it does it with a realism that avoids tyranny.

First the Bible shows us where we came from and where

we are going. It highlights something of the path or the pilgrimage on the way to our destination. We see these themes reflected in key texts: Genesis 1–2, regarding creation; Genesis 12ff., regarding a call to be the people of God; 1 Pet. 2:9–10, where "outsiders" are included in the covenant; and Revelation 21, where the final destiny of the redeemed is described. These and other passages give us grounds for identity and hope.

Second the Bible states norms for belief and behavior: Gen. 1:28–30, the rules for the newly-created humans; Genesis 12ff., the commands to Abraham, developed further in such disparate commands as Deut. 6:4–5 and Exod. 34:26; the Sermon on the Mount (Matthew 5–7); or many of the New Testament epistles (Eph. 4:25–32) give specific directives or norms for living.

Finally, we are reminded of the gravity of the stated norms and how they may serve as "checks and balances" for one's conformity to the norms. Whether in parable form (2 Sam. 12:1–14; Luke 10:30–37), directives (Josh. 24:19), or corrective statements (Gal. 2:11–12), one is confronted by the call to live with honesty and integrity of heart. The Scripture is an authority in that it is intended to produce *metanoia*, repentance, in those who hear it as "the Word of God."

CHAPTER THREE

Revelation and Inspiration

BASIC TO HERMENEUTICAL endeavor in the Bible is the question of the nature of divine revelation. The approaches taken are "largely determined by the concept of the character and the nature of the biblical record as they are related to and understand of revelation."[1] Until one settles this primary question it appears difficult to approach the work of biblical hermeneutics.

The nature of revelation

The term revelation has reference to God's disclosure or revelation of himself and his will to mankind. Theologians often refer to "special revelation," with its culmination in the Incarnation (namely, "the Word became flesh, and dwelt among us, and we beheld His glory," John 1:14 NASB), as opposed to "general revelation" which is God's disclosure in nature and history.

In a wider context we are involved with the task of approaching "truth" (epistemology). For example, is there a difference between how a prophet and a philosopher approach truth? These two questions will serve as models for thinking about truth as disclosure and truth as discovery, respectively. Some biblical ways of stating the contrast are observed in the following statements from the NASB:

> Now it came about in the thirtieth year ... the word of the Lord came expressly to Ezekiel the priest, son of Buzi, in the land of the Chaldeans by the river Chebar (Ezek. 1:1, 3).

> Surely the Lord God does nothing unless He reveals His secret counsel.
> To his servants the prophets (Amos 3:7).

> I was in the Spirit on the Lord's day, and I heard behind me a loud voice ... saying, "write in a book what you see" (Rev. 1:10f.).

> And, of God's servant Moses, it was said: "With him I speak mouth to mouth,
> Even openly, and not in dark sayings,
> And he beholds the form of the Lord" (Num. 12:8).

By way of contrast the philosopher makes use of his highest faculty, "reason," to discover truth. He seeks for it within the whole range of human life and the universe about us. To seek after God, to search for the highest good, and to penetrate mysteries of life, are all quests of philosophic minds. In the Bible we hear allusions to this as well:

> That they should seek God, if perhaps they might grope for Him and find Him (Acts 17:27).

> The Greeks search for wisdom (1 Cor. 1:22).

> These are matters which have, to be sure, the appearance of wisdom in self-made religion and self-abasement and severe treatment of the body (Col. 2:23; compare v. 8).

It would be unwise to set revelation and discovery, or faith and reason, in mutually exclusive categories, however. The latter element in each case is quite legitimate, indeed required by the former. The God who reveals himself to us calls us to seek him that we might find him. The challenge to faith is to love the Lord with all our minds and to think God's thoughts after him. So it is not a question of disparate elements but of the proper perspective or relationship with regard to the two.

With such a proper balance in hand, let us begin with questions that theologians raise when referring to some aspects of revelation: Is it propositional? Is it personal? Did it come (primarily) through historical events? How is it related to the words and the message of the Bible? This easily moves into questions regarding the so-called inspiration of the Bible; such as, does inspiration guarantee the trustworthiness of every word? Is the Bible inerrant? Are there various levels of inspiration in the Bible? Does inspiration reside in the writer, the writing, or the total process that ends in the formation of the canon of Scripture?

What is propositional revelation? The question can be misleading if the term "propositional" is used only to refer to sentences or statements logically formed. This would raise problems with certain types of literary forms such as parabolic or poetic statements. Further the issue of whether a proposition states only a timeless truth (that is, one not bound or limited by historical or temporal contexts) has been a source of controversy among theologicans and philosophers.

A formal definition of "propositional revelation" has been worded as follows: "that God supernaturally communicated his revelation to chosen spokesmen in the express form of cognitive truths, and that the inspired prophetic-apostolic proclamation reliably articulates these truths in sentences that are not internally contradictory."[2] This is not to distinguish the idea from divine self-revelation, for God reveals himself in what is given in rational forms. Nor does it deny various literary forms (parables, poetry, letters, etc.) but simply affirms that truth conveyed has conceptual adequacy.

P. Helm has analyzed the problem of defining this Word, discerning the following factors:[3]

(1) "Proposition" may simply indicate the meaning or sense of a sentence; that is, two different sets of words may be used to indicate the same truth. Thus they have the same "propositional content." To say, "Edinburgh is the second-largest city in Scotland," is not in contradiction with, "The capital of Scotland is its second largest city." The two propositions have the same meaning.

(2) "Proposition" may refer to a set of words which will vary in meaning depending on the grammatical context. "He

is coming" may be an assertion; or, if within a larger unit, "If he is coming I shall leave," is no assertion at all but an utterance of an intelligent person.

(3) When some theologians deny that the Bible is propositional revelation, what they are really objecting to is "revealed *assertions,* i.e. true propositions revealed by God." Such assertions are rejected because they involve what would be called "timeless" or "unhistorical" assertions.

(4) Few would be willing to opt for understanding biblical statements apart from consideration of time, location, and historical circumstance. If we mean by "timeless" something that is generally true or applicable anywhere, such as proverbs, we come to a question that must be decided by hermeneutics, not decided ahead of time. Further, to deny timelessness or historicity completely would deny that anything could be revealed about God's essential character.

(5) There are some statements which are clearly tensed; that is, they describe a kind of action within time. To say "God delivered Israel from bondage in Egypt" or "Christ died for our sins" would be to say something with specific temporal and historical boundaries.

(6) A false dichotomy is presented by the objection that God reveals himself rather than propositions. There need not be a disjunction between "believing a proposition and believing a person if the proposition is taken to be the assertion of some person."

Thus, while we may talk about sentences our main concern is the reality to which we are pointed. If the proposition is asserted by some person, one whom we can trust, there is not a necessary antithesis between believing a proposition and believing a person. If God says, "Hear, and your soul shall live" (Isa. 55:3), to believe that God has said, "your soul shall live" is to believe God who has made the assertion. Whatever revealed propositions there are, they ought to be regarded as objects to which we give our attention, not the objects themselves of our religious belief.

Underlying this question about "propositional" revelation

is another important issue. Does revelation consist in "propositions revealed" or (as an opposing idea) "divine acts upon which we reflect." D. B. Knox sees the latter as going back to F. D. Maurice and C. Gore and put into a famous statement by W. Temple: "There is no such thing as revealed truth. There are truths of revelation...propositions which express the result of correct thinking concerning revelation; but they are not themselves directly revealed" (from his *Nature, Man and God*, p. 317). Knox argues that the biblical view of revelation, which is essentially propositional, is established in two ways:[4] (1) how the Bible describes revelation; and (2) by examining the biblical data to discern its nature. In the first case, he cites the use of the term "oracles" (see Rom. 3:2, Acts 7:38, Heb. 5:12, 1 Pet. 4:11) as meaning "a revelational utterance" or "a revealed truth." While the expressions involved may describe an event or a concept, in both cases the words form propositions (revealed).[5] Usually in the Bible the expression is "the oracles of God" and is a general way of indicating a divine saying. It also appears to include the divine acts of salvation (see Heb. 1:1, 5:12).[6] In the second case, Knox notes that many "facts" come in propositions—our knowledge of God and ourselves; or, heaven and hell. Visions are described in propositions (for example, Isa. 1:1, 2 Chron. 32:32).

Thus Knox argues that a denial of this viewpoint is tantamount to "reducing" the Bible to the same level as the witness of the Church and of the human spirit or reason. In that case revelation will be reshaped by each interpreter of the act/event. But unless God interprets, the happening will not be revelation.

In contrast to the position represented by Knox, others strongly contend for revelation through history, whether "the acts of God" (as G. E. Wright and R. Fuller) or "salvation-history" (O. Cullmann). "Is it true," asks J. Barr, "that the biblical evidence, and the evidence of the Old Testament in particular, fits with and supports the assertion that 'history' is the absolutely supreme milieu of God's revelation?"[7] While not dissenting completely, he points his readers to the wisdom literature (Proverbs, Ecclesiastes, and some Psalms), asking whether God's "acts" are here a central foundation for our knowledge of him? Even in the narratives of the Exodus there are indications of God's free communication with men; conversations (as in Exodus 3) are pre-conditions of the acts of God.

For many, a possible response to Barr's critique is that the revelation of God is Jesus Christ, meaning that our views of how God communicates proceed from the center of Jesus Christ. Yet this view will not explain how the revelation has come "in Christ." Is it mainly in his words, his works, his death, or his resurrection? And how does this view relate to the great variety of situations in the Old Testament which were understood as revelatory? One might reply that the Old Testament traditions point to, or lead on to, Christ. In this response the Old Testament is "soteriologically functional."[8]

A curious disjunction of the two elements in this last position occur in the recent "Chicago Statement on Biblical Hermeneutics,"[9] dated November, 1982. Two articles are quoted here:

> Article III.   WE AFFIRM that the Person and work of Jesus Christ are *the central focus of the entire Bible.* WE DENY that any method of interpretation which rejects or obscures the Christ-centeredness of Scripture is correct.

> Article VI.   WE DENY that, while Scripture is able to make us wise unto salvation, *biblical truth should be defined in terms of that function.*

One may wonder, then, at the wisdom of trying to insist on posing the question in this form—is revelation "propositional" or "personal"? Should we insist on an either/or situation, especially if our basic motivation is to strengthen some assumption about the specific nature of revelation. What does Scripture itself show us about the problem? Do we not see revelation "in many and various ways" (Heb. 1:1)? God's speaking was marked by diversity both in location and method of disclosure. There were visions, dreams, symbols, angels, natural events, prophetic ecstasy, the pillar of fire, or even face to face.[10] There were typical ordinances, declarations of "the word of the Lord," and interpretations of the circumstances surrounding national prosperity and distress.[11] Revelation, then, was limited neither to one time, place, nor form. It was full of variety, both propositional and personal, yet entirely stemming from the single Source—it was God who "uttered his voice."

In a valuable essay, E. Ellis has faced the question of some of the challenges to biblical authority (whether moral, theological, literary-historical or scientific) with three questions bearing on the nature of divine revelation:[12]

(1) What is the nature of revelation: divine truth available or divine truth mediated?

(2) What is the locus of biblical revelation: the original words or the message that resides both in the autograph or in any reasonably accurate copy?

(3) What is the scope of revelation in Scripture: what it touches or what it teaches?

We shall examine his responses to each question in turn. First we have Jesus' attitude toward, and use of, Scripture as a model. Notice his appeals to biblical texts: "Have you not read?" (Matt. 19:4); "It is written" (Matt. 4:4, 7, 10); the full accomplishment of the law (Matt. 5:18); or, to his opponents, "You are wrong, because you know neither the Scriptures nor the power of God" (Matt. 22:29). While God's words are spoken by God's prophets, there is no simple identification of the words of the Bible with the word of God (the *graphe*, "the writing"). We observe both Jesus and the apostles sometimes distinguishing a "Spirit-carried message" and a "dead letter." Earlier we have noted the condemnation of tradition (whenever it transgresses or makes void the word of God; for example, Matt. 15:3–6; Mark 7:6–13); or Paul's words about reading Moses (that is, the Torah, the divine instruction), but having "a veil . . . over their minds" (2 Cor. 3:15). Thus Scripture seems to indicate that revelation is truth mediated, both personal and propositional in form. There is the "Word of God hidden" and "the Word of God revealed." Revelation is not static or abstract. It is dynamic and personally directed.

Second, we see in the New Testament an emphasis on the meaning of Old Testament texts, not upon a certain text-type (whether Hebrew, Greek, or Aramaic). While this theme will be considered at some length in the next chapter (the New Testament use of the Old Testament), we may take an example here. In Rom. 11:26 Paul wrote: "As it is written, 'The Deliverer will come from Zion, he will banish ungodliness from Jacob.'" The Hebrew text of Isa. 59:20 reads: "And he will come to Zion as Redeemer, to those in Jacob who turn from transgression, says the Lord." Here Paul has followed the Greek version (LXX) of the passage that emphasizes the divine action ("he will banish ungodliness from Jacob") in contrast to the Hebrew text that emphasizes the human action ("those in Jacob who turn from transgression").

Notice that Paul prefaces his quotation from, or use of, the Greek text, with the standard formula "as it is written." It appears that in his selection of a version of the Old Testament texts, or a rendering of his own, Paul regarded his citation as thereby more accurately rendering the true meaning of the Scripture.[13] This type of practice by the New Testament writers appears to demonstrate that "the Word-of-God character of Scripture, its infallible and revelational character, was always bound up with its meaning and, we may add, its meaning for the contemporary hearer."[14]

Third, on the sensitive issue of whether the scope of revelation is what Scripture touches or what it teaches, we ask why should there be tension between those who emphasize revelation as "encounter" and those who defend revelation as "propositional." If either side is concerned enough to defend Scripture from any kind of error, it is clear that human error may be no less present in one's psyche than in one's mind.

To argue that there is no distinction between what Scripture touches and what it teaches has led to many further problems. If one attempts to establish the accuracy of all historical and scientific items in Scripture by appealing to the latest scientific evidence or viewpoint, a reading of church history will easily demonstrate the risks involved. To tie the latest scientific view to Scripture can lead to worse problems (whether a view of the character of our solar system based on Josh. 10:12–13, or belief in spontaneous generation based on Judg. 14:8).

Without doubt, to argue that what the Bible teaches or asserts is central and what it touches is incidental and no part of the teaching, will involve risks as well. Yet if one proceeds with integrity, this approach seems reasonable. It relates to the understanding of "the Word of God" that the New Testament affirms and practices; it delivers us from seeing the Bible in the abstract, stemming from a philosophical deductive approach rather than from a study of the data of Scripture; and it gives the biblical scholar freedom to pursue the task of reverent study without being taken up with a plethora of various minutiae, scientific theories, and the like.

The character of inspiration

When we turn to the related theme of the inspiration of the Bible, we are faced with two basic questions: (1) In asserting the Bible's inspiration, what are we required to affirm about the content of the Bible as a whole and of its constituent parts? and (2) In claiming the Bible is thus authoritative, what are we required to affirm about its continuing authority in any particular word or text of Scripture?[15]

To be sure, for many centuries we have had an inspired form of the Scriptures in the canon. This is the final form which inspiration has taken. Yet, for many, the question relates to an earlier point in time—either to the time of the writer(s) of any biblical book, or to the original written product itself, or even to the whole process that led to the canonical form.[16]

Basically there have been two approaches to this theme—

the deductive and the inductive. Essentially the former begins with certain affirmations about the nature of God. Divine righteousness and truthfulness are applied to God's revelatory work, particularly special revelation as seen in Scripture. Thus if God be true his way is perfect, and "the law of the Lord is perfect." E. J. Young asserted that Scripture was "the Word of God written and *hence,* infallible, free entirely from the errors which adhere to mere human compositions" (italics mine).[17] The Bible will then be read with this as a controlling datum.

Induction, on the other hand, often begins with the basic idea, "God has spoken in Scripture," then proceeds to read the Bible to see what the internal data indicate, taking the specific phenomena seriously.[18] Sometimes in this view greater emphasis is placed upon the authority, even the infallibility of Scripture, with less use of the qualifying phrase (as in Young's statement), "free entirely from the errors which adhere to mere human compositions."

For the deductivist, appeal is made to some key texts in the Bible that are understood to affirm a high view of biblical inspiration, even to the extent of "free from all error." Such statements as 2 Tim. 3:16, 2 Pet. 1:20–21, John 10:35, and Matt. 5:18 are standard illustrations: "All Scripture is God-breathed" NIV; "men moved by the Holy Spirit spoke from God" NASB; "the Scripture cannot be broken" NASB; and, "not an iota, not a dot, will pass from the law until all is accomplished" RSV. It appears to follow from all these statements that the character attributed to the Scriptures comes from being "God-breathed"—thus it is authoritative and certain to come to complete fulfillment.

Probably the strongest arguments for a high view of inspiration—what is often called "verbal inspiration"—can be mounted from statements found in the Gospels. Inspiration is attributed to the writings (rather than the writers, as such), and to the words that make them up.[19] "Scripture was Scripture to Christ because it has God as its primary author—in a way that no other writing has."[20]

Does this high view of inspiration necessarily include what is called "inerrancy"? The term has been much discussed. One standard definition is that "*inerrancy* signifies the quality of being free from all falsehood or mistake and so safeguards the truth that Holy Scripture is entirely true and trustworthy in all its assertions."[21] P. D. Feinberg has proposed the following:[22] "Inerrancy means that when all facts are known, the Scriptures in their original autographs and properly interpreted will be shown to be wholly true in everything that they affirm, whether that has to do with doctrine or morality or with the social, physical, or life sciences." These statements should serve to give some samplings of basic deductivist approaches to the theme of inspiration of Scripture. They generally represent writers of a philosophical or theological approach to the subject. Now let us turn for some samplings of a generally inductivist approach, from biblical scholars or exegetes.

In an essay published in 1959 that anticipates later developments in the 1970s and onward, E. F. Harrison affirmed that "unquestionably the Bible teaches its own inspiration" because "it is the Book of God."[23] He grants that the Bible says nothing precise about its own inerrancy, nor does the Bible's claim to inspiration require us to hold to inerrancy (though, he adds, this is a natural accompaniment to full inspiration; that is, the divine character of Scripture). In a far different spirit from many writers on the subject, he states: "Every man must be persuaded in his own mind."

Harrison candidly admits it is perplexing to find various problems in the Bible. There are conflicts in numerical figures in parallel passages of the same event: 2 Sam. 10:18—700 charioteers killed; 1 Chron. 19:18—7,000 charioteers killed (was this a scribal attempt to glorify the reign of David and the kingdom of Judah?); 1 Kings 4:26—40,000 stalls of horses; 2 Chron. 9:25—4,000 stalls of horses. (Here in Chronicles the figures are reduced.)

There are occasional "verbal contradictions" in the gospel accounts. Compare Mark 6:8 with Matt. 10:9f. and Luke 9:3

(the disciples were to carry a staff in Mark yet in the others they were prohibited from carrying a staff. All passages apparently refer to the same occasion).

Sometimes there are problems of sources, as in the stories about Abraham. According to Gen. 11:26, 32, and 12:4, Terah, Abraham's father, lived 60 years after his son left Haran. According to Acts 7:4, however, Abraham left Haran after his father died. (Where did Stephen get his data? It is interesting to see that Philo, in his *Migration of Abraham* 177, gives the same information as seen in Acts. Did both draw from some lost Greek version?)

Again we see problems with citations of the Old Testament in the New. Matthew 27:9 asserts that a passage spoken "through Jeremiah the prophet" is now fulfilled. Yet the words are found instead in Zech. 11:12–13! (Was this "a slip of the pen?" as one has asked. Or was there a "sourcebook" of quotations under the name of Jeremiah?)

These phenomena which present difficulties cannot be dismissed nor should they be underrated. They stand side by side with the Bible's claims to be "God-breathed." Thus the scholar or student may ask if the inspired character of Scripture necessitates inerrancy? Some will say that inspiration "rather defines the relation of the Scripture to God. It points to the source of the Scripture,"[24] rather than to a property inherent in the text. Others, like L. Morris, will acknowledge the presence of problem passages, but prefer a way of looking at the Bible which holds to its "full authority" yet does not bog down in defending minor points.[25] The final authority of Scripture, he argues, is not "paper and printer's ink," but the Spirit speaking through the Bible. The Bible is meant to give us a true knowledge of God.

At this point we have come nearly full circle, from beginning with the words of 2 Tim. 3:16 and seeing it as an endorsement of "all Scripture," meaning every word in the Bible as such, to seeing that inspiration is related to "making us wise unto salvation." It moves the argument from the verbally harmonious character of Scripture to the undistorted sense (or message) of Scripture. The dilemma lies unresolved, but some find a provisional answer in following the pattern seen in Scripture itself. To this we turn briefly.

To see how Scripture functions as "authority in practice" is a helpful model for those who hold a high view of inspiration but have genuine doubts about the validity of the inerrancy issue. Scripture interpreted is authoritative Scripture. It is the use of the Word of God that brings home its impact. Notice Jesus' selective interpretation of such texts as Isa. 61:1–2, where he separated "the day of vengeance" from the other elements of the passages (see Luke 4:16–27), or his interpretation of aspects of the Law in Matt. 5:38–39 or Mark 10:2–12, where he set aside parts of the Scriptural texts, or denied the relevancy of certain statements for his own day. J. Dunn notes that in each of these instances "Jesus did not regard the Old Testament text in question as having an absolute, infallible (= unrefusable) authority," but he saw them in their relevance to the historical situations in which they were first spoken.[26] The same kind of approach can be observed in the use of Scripture by the earliest churches (see Rom. 1:17 in its use of Hab. 2:4; Rom. 10:6–10 in its use of Deut. 30:11–14, or Mark 7:19 in its displacement of food laws because of Jesus' teaching).

The point for our study here is twofold: (1) determine the historical sense of the text; that is, ask what the writer intended the reader to hear; and (2) realize that God continues to speak through Scripture; that is, both in its initial intended sense and new ways in which the Holy Spirit applies the Word of God.

CHAPTER FOUR

The New Testament Use of the Old

THE OLD TESTAMENT was the Bible of Jesus and the early Church. They believed it, quoted it, and interpreted it. Without question, the primary meaning or significance of the Scriptures was, for them, twofold: (1) its witness to the Christ, seen to be Jesus of Nazareth; and (2) its value for "instruction, that by steadfastness and by the encouragement of the scriptures we might have hope" (Rom. 15:4). The former was a word of salvation (compare 2 Tim. 3:15); God had fulfilled his promise to send a Deliverer to Zion; the latter was a word of direction, for God intended that his people be guided in life by the Word that is "a lamp for the feet and a light for the path" (Ps. 119:105).

Current views of the relationship

Our particular interest here is to see how the New Testament used the Old, in terms of attitudes toward and methods of drawing upon, exegeting and applying its message. First, what current views have been expressed regarding the relationship between the Old Testament and the New Testament? The answers have been varied indeed. R. E. Murphy has surveyed the ongoing debate, which we summarize here:[1]

(1) For R. Bultmann, there is "complete discontinuity" between the two; the ideas of the covenant, the Kingdom of God and the People of God have been shattered historically. He calls them "an inner contradiction with the Old Testament."

(2) For F. Baumgartel, the Old Testament is "a witness out

of a non-Christian religion," yet the theme "I am the Lord thy God" finds realization in the New.

(3) For W. Zimmerli, C. Westermann, and others, there is a basic bond between the two in the promise/fulfillment theme. It is rooted in history and is clarified by the divine word of interpretation.

(4) For B. W. Anderson, there is a continuity/discontinuity theme illustrated from Jer. 31:31–34 where "the covenant is now made a promise of salvation." Between the two there is the same purpose (relationship to God), the same people (of God), and the same Law (Torah).

(5) For J. Dillenberg, "revelational discernment" is advocated, meaning the New Testament "must be used as the angle of vision" to properly understand the Old, showing the fulfillment of the promise in Christ.

(6) For J. L. McKenzie, the correlation of the Old and the New is related to the understanding and needs of the times, thus an existential approach is valid in exegesis. The Old Testament shows man as sinner under divine judgment, thus open to divine salvation.

(7) For W. Eichrodt, the typological approach is valid, both by way of similarity and contrast. The persons, institutions, and events of the Old are "divinely established models or pre-representations of corresponding realities" in the salvation history of the New.

(8) For P. Grelot, the Old is preparatory and figurative with respect to the New. He sees the Law and the history of Israel as illustrations of the progress of salvation through all the sufferings and judgments in Israel, toward the paradox of the Cross.

In consideration of these viewpoints, certain elements are clarified by Murphy.[2] Fundamental in Christian belief is that the Father of Jesus Christ is the same God as in the Old Testament. This means that the Testaments are related. Yet we perceive the presence of continuity and discontinuity; there is still the "old" and the "new." Do we then read from the Old into the New (continuity)?—or, from the New into the Old (discontinuity)? How do we reach basic agreement on "unity" (and what do we mean by the idea)? For some, the most convincing category is promise/fulfillment, a theme present in many current studies of the problem. Israel has had experience with a saving God, and we may see this theme elaborated in the New Testament through the general typology and fuller perspective that meets us there. The idea of promise/fulfillment is to be found in the Old Testament itself, and does provide a continuity with the New. Yet it is open-ended, looking toward the future. Fulfillment is "the flowering of what was set in motion by the word (or event) and fulfillment." One needs to be aware of the objective relation between the two Testaments, not only an existential appropriation. The plane of history is important, and so is the theme of promise.

On the one hand, the New Testament gives guidelines for interpretation of the Old; on the other, it is not definitive in details. Thus various interpreters react to the Old Testament as they perceive it to be. In controlling typological insights, the New Testament plays an important role. Otherwise interpretations easily become arbitrary.

Finally, there is an unfolding character to the Old Testament revelation. This may be seen in both the development of a religious vocabulary and religious ideas.

Jewish interpretation of the Old Testament

We must begin with some consideration of the Jewish use and interpretation of the Old Testament as seen in the work of the scribes, the Septuagint (LXX), and the writing of the Qumran sectaries. Further, the rationale for this part of the study is the belief that the New Testament writers, being Jews (with the possible exception of Luke) were both familiar with and employed the same basic approaches to the Old Testament current in their culture.

Interpretation among Jewish scholars appears to stem from the work of Ezra, "a scribe skilled in the law of Moses" (Ezra

BRITISH ISLES NAZARENE LIBRARY 16076

7:6). Under his direction, the Law was brought before the restored assembly of Israel, many of whom had returned from exile in Babylon.[3] On that occasion, we are told, "they read from the book, from the law of God, clearly [or *with interpretation*]; and they gave the sense, so that the people understood the reading" (Neh. 8:8 RSV). This refers to a rendering of the Hebrew law into the vernacular Aramaic, so that the people would hear the divine instructions in their own tongue.

Ezra's importance stems from his arrival during the time of a receding prophetism which was replaced with emphasis upon religious precepts and practices.[4] Not only was the Law established as a base for Jewish life but various enactments were propounded as the need arose. Thus we see the rise of "the traditions" that were to play such a major role in Jewish life. The so-called "Great Synagogue" may have grown out of this precedent. We think of it as a kind of council that made regulations as were thought to be needed and passed them on with their authority. From Ezra and the men of the Great Synagogue these regulations were passed along to the Scribes and the Rabbis.[5]

In the Book of Sirach (or Ecclesiasticus—a book in the so-called Apocrypha of the Old Testament, dated in the second century B.C.) we read the teachings of an early biblical scholar and one learned in the Torah. Some light is shed on the instruction of scribes in those days. It included interpretation of the Pentateuchal laws, along with common law, ordinances, and decrees that had been passed down by earlier authorities.

Late in the second century B.C., the Scribes presumably gained support from the Pharisees, a group that had arisen as champions of tradition. They attached great importance to the exact interpretation and application of the laws of the Jews. In contrast to the Sadducees, they expounded and defended traditional rules and observances which had no direct biblical authority. G. F. Moore sees the primary distinction between these two parties in the doctrine of revelation:

Scripture alone for the Sadducees; Scripture and Tradition for the Pharisees.[6]

With the activity of the Pairs, rabbis between the time of Simeon the Just (second century B.C.) and the reign of Herod the Great (37–34 B.C.), the chain of tradition was continued. During the days of Rabbis Shammai and Hillel, the last of the Pairs, certain hermeneutical rules for a system of deduction and analogy, called Hillel's Seven Rules (or *Middot*),[7] were propounded. Generally, Hillel was more lenient in his interpretations, Shammai more strict; Hillel sometimes departed from the literal sense of the text, Shammai tended to be more literal.

Highly important here is that the application of Hillel's hermeneutical principles was intended to establish the harmony between tradition and Scripture.[8] He projected the practice of interpreting the text into a prominent position in rabbinic methodology and was able to show by use of his rules that his conclusions were at one with the authoritative tradition.[9]

For the rabbis Scripture was homogeneous; it contained no contradictions, and differences were only apparent. Most vital was their view that Scripture, every word of which was believed to be of divine origin, teaches religion, and that the whole of religion is contained therein. The exegete, therefore, is to discover, elucidate, and apply the text to life. Moore calls this view "the first principle of Jewish hermeneutics."[10]

The profound reverence for Scripture found among Jewish interpreters led them to emphasize the letter of the text; the desire for more truth spurred them in the search for hidden meanings. C. H. Toy gives a summary principle: "Every sentence and every word of the Scripture was credited with any meaning it could possibly be made to bear; and the interpreter selected the literal or the allegorical sense, or any other that suited his argument."[11] Sometimes it was a single word that was significant. In a passage in the Babylonian Talmud, a question arises about the meaning of a reference to the angel Gabriel in Dan. 9:21: "The man Gabriel . . . being caused to fly in a flight," is interpreted, "The meaning is: Michael covered the distance in one flight, without any stop, whereas Gabriel had to make two flights, resting in between. This is inferred from the fact that the word *fly* occurs twice."[12]

On other occasions it was the numerical value of the Hebrew letter. In the incident of Abraham pitching his tent between Bethel and Ai (Gen. 12:8), "Bethel" minus "Ai" = 358, which is also the value of "Messiah." The tent was halfway between = 179, which is the value of Paradise, "the garden of Eden." Thus the conclusion: "In fact, after this life of making a mockery of idols and shattering them, Abraham comes to the place which is the garden of Eden, on the way which is the way of Messiah."[13] This method of interpreting Scripture assumes that the written text was fixed by God from the very beginning. Thus even to vary the text by a jot or a tittle would bring collapse, and only a story would remain.

Scribes distinguished two methods of interpretation; namely, *peshat* or "plain (meaning)" and *derash* or "exposition" that attempted to derive religious or social ethics from the text. The most important form of interpretation at this early period was a detailed application of the written Torah to new circumstances of Jewish life in the Graeco-Roman world.[14]

By means of *halakah* ("binding rule," a prescriptive statement) and *haggadah* ("narration," a theological or moral lesson), the Rabbis pursued their exegesis of the traditional materials. Together with these, *midrash* was the higher exegesis of Scripture because it was derived from the rules of the unwritten law (oral Torah).[15] For example, in Deut. 27:6: "You shall build an altar to the Lord your God of unhewn [or *whole*] stones," the first of Hillel's seven rules (see note 6 for this chapter) was applied:

> This means stones that establish peace (šalôm). See, the conclusion *a minori ad maius* applies. If God said, with reference to the stones of the altar, which neither see nor hear

nor speak, because they establish peace between Israel and their Father in heaven, 'Thou shalt not lift up iron upon them' (Deut. 27:5), how much more does it apply to him who establishes peace between two men, or between a man and his wife, or between two towns, or, two nations, or two governments, or two families, that no punishment shall come upon him.[16]

Examples of this type of exegesis can be seen in the New Testament—in Mark 2:23–28, concerning David and the Son of man; in Heb. 9:13–14, with regard to the blood of Jewish sacrifices and the blood of Christ; and, in Rom. 5:12–21, concerning Adam and Christ.

The Septuagint itself was a rendering of the Hebrew text of the Old Testament. It varies in many places from what is known as the Masoretic text of the Hebrew Bible (a text of the Hebrew Bible preserved by Jewish scholars during the Middle Ages), but not always due to careless scribal copying. Recent studies have shown an autonomy of the LXX; that is, it is a piece of Greek literature in its own right, and one that held its place in the early church as "the inspired Scriptures."[17]

Certain tendencies appear in the LXX rendering of the text.[18] Some are anthropomorphisms that soften the impact of the Hebrew reading (in Exod. 24:10 it reads, "they saw the place where the God of Israel stood" for "they saw the God of Israel"; in Isa. 42:13 it reads, "destroys war" for God as "a man of war"). In other cases the text is universalized, spiritualized (as in Amos 9:11–12, where it reads "the rest of mankind" instead of the "Edom" of the Hebrew text), or certain Greek ethical/metaphysical influences have appeared (as in Prov. 13:10, "with those who take advice is wisdom"). Other well-known changes are the use of "virgin" (*parthenos*) rather than the more general "young woman" (*almah*) in Isa. 7:14 (compare Matt. 1:23) or the insertion of the words "not" in the second and third clauses of Isa. 8:14.

The key representative of Jewish scholarship outside Palestine in the first century was Philo of Alexandria. He is best known for allegorizing the text—for a multitude of reasons. Possibly a concrete example will speak for itself. In his treatise "On the Posterity of Cain and His Exile,"[19] he begins "And Cain went out from the face of God" (Gen. 4:16). He raises the question whether we ought to take the statements figuratively, "since the impression made by the words in their literal sense is greatly at variance with truth." The problem is, does God have a face? And how can we remove ourselves from God? His conclusion is, "the only thing left for us to do is to make up our minds that none of the propositions put forward is literally intended and to take the path of figurative interpretation so dear to philosophical souls" (p. 331). (He means by "philosophical" the quest for the truth or reality underlying interpretations of God and divine things.)

Finally, among Jewish interpretations, we look to the Qumran scholars. While the exegetical approaches of the Qumran sect (a community of priests and scholars located near the northwest shore of the Dead Sea) included some allegorical elements, the main thrust of their methodology was "historical." They believed Scripture applied to their own group and the historical circumstances of their own time. The Old Testament was interpreted in the light of recent events, and the present was a doorstep into eschatological time—the End, in which God's purposes would progressively come to fulfillment. God had revealed his will to the prophets, yet these things were given in a mysterious form. With particular reference to the time of the End, the community at Qumran believed that God had given the solution to "the teacher who expounds the Law aright."[20]

Their usual method of interpretation, called *pesher* "that is" or "this refers to," was used to bring the words of Scripture into conjunction with their own circumstances and to give anticipation of a near end to current history— anticipating the forty-year period of "Messianic woes."[21] It is in their now-famous commentary on the Old Testament prophecy of Habakkuk that their exegesis is best illustrated. In this text they come closest to an approach taken in the

New Testament. The Scriptures contain a divine mystery (*raz*); the *pesher* is an interpretation given by divine illumination (see Dan. 2:30, where both words occur). They saw themselves in the tradition of Daniel who had been given wisdom, revealing to him the "deep and mysterious things" (Dan. 2:20–23). The first century Jewish historian Josephus said of Daniel that "Daniel spoke with God, for he was not only wont to prophesy future things, as did the other prophets, but he also fixed the time at which these things would come to pass."[22]

Any number of prophecies were brought together by these scholars to bear upon their present plight under the Romans. Referred to as the *kittim*, the Romans thus fulfilled Balaam's *kittim* (Num. 24:24); Isaiah's Assyrian (Isa. 10:5; 31:8); Ezekiel's Gog (Ezek. 38:1ff); and Habakkuk's Chaldeans (Hab. 1:6). Bruce comments, "All this exegesis involves the atomization of the biblical text," but the coherence was found not there but "in the situation to which the biblical text pointed."[23]

The other aspect of Qumram interpretation concerned the relevance of the Torah (the laws of Israel as a rule of life). Their interpretation and enforcement of the various laws tended to be severe and exclusive. As there is "but one God and one truth, there can be but one way."

The basic principles of Qumran exegesis have been summed up as follows:[24]

(1) God revealed his purpose to his servants the prophets, but his revelation, particularly respecting the time of fulfillment, was imparted (or, revealed) to the Teacher of Righteousness (or the Righteous Teacher).

(2) The prophets' words all refer to the time of the end.

(3) The time of the end is at hand. (See such prophecies as contained in Num. 24:17; Deut. 18:15; Isa. 10:27ff.; 31:8; Mic. 1:6; Nah. 2:11ff.; Hab. 1:6; Ezek. 28:1ff.)

Such interpretation does damage to any genuine historical study of the texts and does away with their relevance to the people to whom they were addressed. The Assyrians, the

Babylonians, or Gog are all made into various "code-names" for the last great oppressive military force in the end time.

The Hebrew Scriptures were the "Bible" of Jesus and his followers. Thus exegesis in the New Testament is mainly concerned with the use of the Old. Since the remainder of this chapter is devoted to this subject, we shall simply do some systematic linking with the previous discussions on rabbinic and Qumran exegesis, thereby raising important issues for further investigation.

There are a number of Jewish methods of interpretation occurring in the New Testament:[25]

(1) The use of allegory. This methodology is relatively rare in the New Testament; some scholars deny that it occurs at all. The single use of the term itself is in Gal. 4:21–31: "Now this is an allegory" (RSV); or "This contains an allegory" (NASB). Allegory is a methodology (as opposed to a literary genre) in which a statement has a deeper, more profound, "spiritualized" sense. Paul's use of the term in Galatians (compare 1 Cor. 5:6–8; 9:8–10; 10:1–11) is much more restrained than the work of Philo of Alexandria or of the Alexandrian scholars of a later period. Paul regards the two women, their two children, and mountains or cities to have meanings beyond the literal. F. Buschsel thinks that Paul's use of this distinctive feature in the exposition of Scriptures is only possible for one living in the time of its fulfillment (compare 1 Cor. 10:11).[26]

(2) The use of *pesher.* In Rom. 10:6–7 Paul cited Deut. 30:11–14, and interpreted it with the words "that is." One will see readily that the historical sense of the words of the text are quite distinct from Paul's use of them. Yet he simply moves from the commandment of God given through Moses to Israel in the wilderness to the message centered in Christ, proclaimed to the Roman church of his day (namely, "the word of faith which we are proclaiming" v. 8).

(3) The principle of less to greater. As we have already alluded to these above, notice examples in Mark 2:23–28; Heb. 9:13–14; and 2 Cor. 3:14–18.

(4) The principle of analogy (common word). The word

"reckoned" in Rom. 4:3 occurs in a quotation of Gen. 15:6. In what sense is the word used? Paul (in vv. 7–8) appeals to another text (Ps. 32:1–2): "Blessed is the man against whom the Lord will not reckon his sin." In the latter text this means to be forgiven or to have one's sins covered (thus Ps. 32:1 in Rom. 4:7). Paul used the latter passage to define the former.

(5) Straightforward interpretation. Here the Old Testament is cited as it says candidly what the New Testament writer desires to assert. There are examples to follow or to avoid— Elijah who prayed (Jas. 5:17–18); Job who endured (Jas. 5:11); Cain who murdered his brother (1 John 3:12); and Esau who profaned his birthright (Heb. 12:16). It is quite plain that one should love both God and one's neighbor (Mark 12:28–34).

Certainly the key characteristic of New Testament interpretation is its Christological dimension. Here appeal is made to prophecy and to typology. Jesus is viewed as the Messiah, not alone on the basis of the life-experiences of the early disciples but because they found the Hebrew Scriptures to be anticipatory; to be full of promise and expectation.

Further, the Old Testament was interpreted with regard to norms and directives for the life of the people of God. Answers to problems they faced, whether social, domestic, ecclesiastical, or whatever, were found through interpreting and applying texts from the Scriptures to themselves. (See Mark 10:2–12 with Deut. 24:1; Gen. 1:27, 2:24; or Acts 15:1–21 with Amos 9:11–12; and 2 Tim. 2:19 with Num. 16:5.)

The use of typology

Another important aspect of the relation between the Old and the New Testaments is the question of the nature and validity of what is called typology. While it has been highly touted by some contemporary writers (W. Eichrodt and M. D. Goulder), it is by no means a recent invention. For one may argue that "it is part of the warp and woof of scripture,"[27] thus making it a significant hermeneutical approach.

Earlier versions of typological interpretation often paid

little attention to the historical framework and character of the Old Testament, thus easily merging into an allegorizing of the Scriptures. This may be seen in the writings of the early Church Fathers, especially in Alexandria. They worked on the principle of a basic unity in Scripture, but this tended to be more of a theological unity (for example, Christological) than one giving attention to historical sequence.

In more recent days, however, this has been largely altered. Since the onset of the modern historical-critical approach to Scripture, there is a clearer emphasis on historical sequence, together with the relationship of the Old Testament to Jesus Christ. H. W. Wolff sees typology as the analogy between Old and New in a historically unique situation—a witness of faith to God's covenant will, based on historical data; a God who chooses and calls to freedom under his Lordship—that has a decisive moment of intensification toward the end of history.[28] Thus typology sees the concrete data of the Old Testament established by historical exegesis valuable for the new, eschatological community of Jesus Christ as it charts its way to specific obedience in history.

A major work examining typology by L. Goppelt, recently published in an English translation, has examined the whole issue in detail.[29] This author sees the Old Testament promises of liberation as "acts of God within history that, at the same time, sovereignly select and go beyond the human political processes of this age" (p. xiv). Goppelt stresses the wide-ranging unity of the New Testament writers' understanding of the Old Testament; that is, it was "the Word of God," as opposed to simply human interpretation. Whatever diversity one does see in the New was due to the various voices speaking differently the message given by the one Spirit.

Goppelt was attempting to respond to the various conclusions of New Testament scholars of the nineteenth and early twentieth centuries on the question of the use of Scriptures in the New. Was it a kind of accommodation to current Jewish methods of interpretation? Was it an allegorical approach? Did it deal mainly with essential ideas apart from details?

Was it a response to a view of Old Testament prophecy? Did history repeat itself, showing a spiritual relationship between persons and events of different periods? Did the redemptive Christ-event fulfill the promises of the Old Testament?

A basic principle of typology is that only "historical facts" (persons, events, and institutions) are material for typological interpretation. These were divinely ordained to be seen as *representative of that which was to come.* Typology shows not only comparison of new with old but, particularly, that redemptive history is the direct and sole foundation of the new. The New Testament refers to a "new creation," to "children of Abraham" and to "an elect nation." On occasion there is an antithesis: Christ is "the second Adam" (see Rom. 5:14ff.); or the new covenant versus the old covenant (for example, 2 Corinthians 3).

Does the view of "history" espoused by a historical-critical methodology invalidate "typology"—if the events of the Old Testament did not really happen as recorded in the narratives, but were reinterpreted as a kerygmatic ("proclaimed") presentation? In view of more recent disciplines such as tradition-history (investigating the development of the Old Testament materials), we still can see dependence on historicity. One may affirm that God fulfilled through Jesus the events which happened to Israel "without being bound to any sequence or development in history"[30]—in the relationship of promise and fulfillment or of type and antitype. If such an approach is granted, typology can lay claim to be legitimate both historically and theologically.

Fundamental to this whole discussion, as noted above, is the question of the relation of the Old Testament to Jesus Christ. Not all are happy to approach it on the basis of typology. It has been carried beyond this to affirm "the real presence of the pre-existent Christ in Old Testament history— or, to be more accurate, the real presence of the pre-existent Jesus."[31] To say with Paul (1 Cor. 10:4) or with John (John 12:37, 41) that Jesus was actually present in the Old Testament scenes, is to depart from a "type"; he himself was there, and so there is no need to speak about types when the reality is present. The key here is the use of the word "Lord" (*Kyrios*) in the texts where identification with Jesus is made (for example, Num. 12:8: "and he has seen the glory of *Kyrios*," compared with the language of Heb. 3:1–6).

Granting that the terms "type" and "antitype" occur in the New Testament (see Rom. 5:14; Heb. 9:24; compare Heb. 8:5; 10:1), Hanson argues they are often used in other than the traditional sense. He sees words like *parabole* (parable) and *semeion* (sign) as more significant. See Heb. 9:9 and 11:19; where the former is used for something symbolic or figurative and Matt. 12:38–41, where the latter is used of "the sign of Jonah."[32]

Thus, we find various levels on which the New Testament interprets the Old by progressively moving away from an emphasis on "history" through: (1) the real presence of Christ in Old Testament history; (2) the approach of prophecy; (3) typology; and (4) allegory.

From a New Testament model, then, we may find an approach to typology that may lead us to consider it a legitimate discipline. The basic idea is correspondence, for God is in control of history.[33] This correspondence is within the historical framework of divine revelation, as opposed to allegorism, which is concerned with hidden meanings beneath the primary and ordinary meanings, and which shows little or no regard for a historical base. The very possibility of types depends on the providence of God; he is related to the people of Israel and their history (compare Exod. 25:8; Deut. 18:15, 18). Thus we may summarize by saying that (1) there must be a basic resemblance or contrast between the type and its antitype; (2) it is a result of the providence of God; and (3) it points beyond itself to some future person, event, or thing.

On a more specific level there is the work of M. Terry.[34] Though old, it is still useful for its detailed illustrations and basic principles for interpreting types:

(1) Look for a central (or "real") point of resemblance

between type and antitype, and avoid all forced analogies. Examples are found in Num. 21:4–9 and John 3:14–15, where we note the relation between the pole and the cross, and the concept of "looking and living"; in Gen. 14:18–20 and Heb. 7:1–3, where Melchizedek appears as both king and priest, the idea of timelessness and perpetuity occur, and both Melchizedek and Christ are a superior to Abraham and the Levitical priesthood.

(2) Points of difference and contrast should be noted along with resemblances. See Heb. 8:1–6, both comparing and contrasting Moses and Christ; and Rom. 5:14–17 on Adam and Christ.

(3) Old Testament types are interpreted fully only in the light of the gospel of Christ. See Heb. 9:6–14, on the sacrifices of the old order contrasted with the new in v. 14 the expression, "How much more"); and Gal. 3:23–25, regarding the character of the Law in contrast to the coming of "the faith."

An obvious question after examining these illustrations concerns a "control" for using typology. What guards against excessive or unwarranted use of the method? For some, every event narrated in the Old Testament history which bore a formal resemblance to something in the New was a type.[35] This obviously left the door completely ajar for the multiplication of types. The opposite approach was to declare as "a rule of thumb" that, unless the New Testament declares something to be a type, we have no warrant for accepting it. By a reading of the New, then, the field of choice was fairly well-circumscribed. A third view suggested there were two varieties of types, called (a) innate because declared by the New Testament, and (b) inferred since justified by the nature of the New Testament use of Old Testament types.

One of the outstanding students of typology in the nineteenth century was P. Fairbairn.[36] He indicated several guidelines in judging the propriety of examples of types in the Old Testament.

(1) Nothing in itself of a forbidden and sinful nature

should be regarded as a type of "the good things" under the gospel; for example, Jacob's deceitful assumption of the blessing while dressed in Esau's garments should not be taken as a type of our receiving the blessing of God in the garments of Jesus Christ.

(2) Not the knowledge possessed by Old Testament people, but the light furnished by the facts of the gospel should be a basis for determining types; for example, that Moses would understand the sign of the burning bush as typifying the great mystery of the Incarnation and the sufferings of Christ.

(3) The religious truths and ideas in typical events and institutions should inform the ground and limit of reference to Christ's kingdom; for example, it was not the material or the shape of the serpent on the pole, but the action of lifting it up that was significant as a type (see John 3:14).

(4) While a type has a single radical meaning, it has many applications, the latter being so due to the close relation between Christ and his people; for example, the Exodus, the manna in the wilderness, etc.

(5) Give due regard to the essential difference between type and antitype; for example, both Israel and Jesus were brought out of Egypt, yet there were many differences temporally and circumstantially.

It appears that great care must be exercised in the "discovery" and use of Old Testament types. The evidence from the New Testament is meager or, at least, limits the use to a few specific types and to a recognition of a central concern reflected in both Testaments—basically a promise/fulfillment theme.[37] The only clear basis are the indications given in the New Testament; beyond this we need to proceed with caution, otherwise the line between a historical approach and allegorization may disappear.

Pauline exegesis

The Pauline exegesis of the Old Testament is widely recognized as a key issue. It is not that Paul's procedures were markedly distinct from other New Testament writers but that a great variety of materials and interpretations are found in his letters. His basic presuppositions would be those shared by his contemporaries; namely, God was sovereign in the affairs of history; the Scriptures were inspired by God; and Jesus was the goal of the history of salvation.[38]

Paul read the Old Testament as prophetic Scripture, pointing toward Christ and the Christian community. Even particular commandments and narratives, such as 1 Cor. 9:9 and 10:1ff., were given prophetic character.[39] Not simply the words but the content of Scripture—its message about Christ—was crucial.

It appears strange to many today that the New Testament writers held the text of the Scriptures in such high esteem (see 2 Tim. 3:16), but they were not limited by the wording in getting at the sense of the text. T. W. Manson has phrased it well:

> For them (Jewish and Christian interpreters) the meaning of the text was of primary importance; and they seem to have had greater confidence than we moderns in their ability to find it. Once found it became a clear duty to express it; and accurate reproduction of the traditional wording of the Divine oracles took second place to publication of what was held to be their essential meaning and immediate application. Odd as it may seem to us, the freedom with which they handled the Biblical text is a direct result of the supreme importance which they attached to it.[40]

A fine example of this very point is to be seen in a comparison of the text of Hab. 2:3–4 with its use in Rom. 1:17, Gal. 3:11 and Heb. 10:37–38. (Particularly in Hebrews, notice the addition of the definite article; thus "the Coming One" is more specifically messianic. Compare Matt. 11:3; and the use of "my righteous one" to refer to the Christian.)

It is now widely recognized that Paul's quotations of Scripture show that he used them to draw out and express the true meaning of the text as he perceived it. E. E. Ellis has shown that many of Paul's quotations vary from the LXX and/or the Hebrew (Masoretic) text—some based on variant textual sources, and *ad hoc* or an interpretative selection from various known texts.[41] The *midrash pesher* type of quotation (see discussion of Qumran exegesis above) seems prominent in Paul's letters. (See 1 Cor. 15:54–55; 2:9, 14:21, and 15:45.)

Paul's use of the Scriptures falls into various groupings, depending on what he was trying to communicate to his readers:[42]

(1) He shows a general prophetic and kerygmatic approach pointing toward the gospel (Rom. 1:2, 3:21; 2 Cor. 6:1–2; and see concerning Adam and Abraham in Rom. 5:14 and Gal. 3:8, respectively).

(2) He appeals to the Scriptures as a source for teaching and edifying the Church in the ethical sphere. It may be specific (2 Cor. 13:1) or general (Rom. 13:8–10). He sometimes criticizes or warns (1 Cor. 10:1–13) and sometimes exhorts (2 Cor. 8:15).

(3) Paul uses the Scriptures to interpret the current historical (or eschatological) situation. The unfolding course of events could be understood in a specific, often Christological sense (see Romans 9–11); in one place "the mystery of Israel" is explained by Rom. 11:34–35, citing Isa. 40:13 and Job 35:7.

(4) He also appeals to the Old Testament "to prove a point"; for example, on wisdom (1 Cor. 1:19, 31; 2:9, 16); regarding the human condition, condemned by the Law (Rom. 3:19–20); regarding freedom (1 Cor. 10:26); concerning spiritual gifts (1 Cor. 14:21); on matters of eschatology (1 Cor. 15:27, 54–55).

With such a varied use of Scripture, is Paul doing violence to the *sensus plenior* of the Old Testament? M. Hooker has asked whether Paul indeed "stuck to Scripture," especially after his advice to the readers at Corinth "not to go beyond what is written" (1 Cor. 4:6).[43] His use of a *pesher* approach to Exodus 34 (in 2 Corinthians 3) appears to violate his own advice. The answer appears quite plain by now—there was much more in Scripture than appeared on the surface or in the letter. The "real message" was hidden until the solution was found in Christ.

To many modern readers this sounds curious, for we have been schooled to pay attention to historical context and the meaning for the original readers. Yet it is the underlying assumptions, not the methods, of Paul that distinguished him from his contemporaries (in Judaism). For most exegetes of the period "the end of the ages (had) come" (1 Cor. 10:11), but Paul saw the Scriptures Christologically, fulfilled in Jesus and his people. In Christ "all the promises of God find their Yes" (2 Cor. 1:20). Scripture witnesses to the consummation of redemption and is based on it.[44]

Basic characteristics of New Testament exegesis

Attention will now be given to further aspects of New Testament interpretation, looking at the basic characteristics of New Testament exegesis in a wider framework.

There has been wide disagreement over the characteristics of the New Testament use of the Old, illustrated by the following citations:

> Perhaps its most conspicuous feature, viz., [is] its disregard of the original context and purpose of the various Old Testament passages with which it deals.[45]

> The distinctive feature of the New Testament use of the Old is the *contextual* exegesis that so often lies behind the citation of individual texts.[46]

The former comment is based on the assumption that, because the Christians believed the Scriptures to be a collection of oracles (inspired writings), the relations between the writings and their original meanings could be disregarded. The latter comment shows the attitude that the New Testament writers did, in fact, have awareness of contextual matters.

A study of the patterns of Old Testament quotations in the New will show that sections of scriptural texts were "understood as *wholes*," and were quoted as "pointers to the whole context" from which they were drawn.[47] There is both a historical awareness and a sense of a theological-redemptive scheme that justifies such a use of the Old Testament.

For example, the lofty poetry of Isaiah 40–66 becomes a "corpus of Gospel *testimonia*," extending from the use of Isaiah 40:3 (concerning John the Baptist) to 65:17 and 66:22 (concerning the anticipated "day of God" in 2 Pet. 3:13 and Rev. 21:1). The lofty figure of "one like a Son of Man" (Dan. 7:13–14) and the Suffering Servant of Isaiah are brought to bear upon the career of Jesus, combining the two into one. The phrase "people of God" in Hosea (see 1:10; 2:23) can be placed upon "the exiles of the Dispersion" of a later day and culture (1 Pet. 2:9–10).

There are exegetical patterns both common and varied among the New Testament writers. It has been noted that in the early New Testament preaching, biblical quotations are found mainly within the mission to the Jews (see Romans, Galatians, also Matthew, John, Hebrews, James, 1 and 2 Peter, and Jude).[48] There is a striking contrast in materials basically directed to Gentiles (see Mark; Luke uses little editorial comment; also 1 and 2 Thessalonians, Colossians, Philemon, and Philippians).

Second, the development of a *pesher* type of exegesis was due to a key interest in showing redemptive fulfillment in Jesus of Nazareth. There is a free use of various textual traditions to this end (for example, Matt. 1:23; 2:15, 18, 23; Acts 3:24; 4:17; 1 Pet. 2:7; 1 Cor. 15:3–5).

Third, there was a view of salvation as history within a framework of two ages—this age and the age to come.[49] The background lay in the Old Testament prophets (compare the apocalyptic writings). Illustrations may be seen in Matt. 3:2–3, 10–12, and Eph. 1:10, in "a divinely-ordered plan" (*oikonomia*).

Basic to New Testament interpretation was Jesus' use of

Scripture. Some of the outstanding features as seen in the Gospels are:

(1) The witness of the Scriptures to him must be perceived through or beyond the letter of the text (John 5:39–40).

(2) The theological realities of the Scriptures must be experienced (Mark 12:24–27).

(3) Whatever the Scripture designs for fulfillment must certainly come to pass (Matt. 5:1–18), especially the Christological anticipations and promises (Luke 24:25–27, 44ff.).

(4) The Scriptures are authoritative as the Word of God (Matt. 4:1–11; John 10:34–36), and they are expounded in their relation to human beings (Mark 1:21–22; Matt. 7:24–29).

(5) There is a dimension of meaning beyond the original context when a similar situation exists (Matt. 21:42–43; 23:38) or when an analogy may be drawn (Matt. 12:38–42).

(6) Not all texts of Scripture are on the same level of importance or relevance; for example, the many commandments may be seen in two (Matt. 22:36–40); or the law of marriage is based on the original conception (Gen. 2:24), not on a concession made because of "hardness of heart" (Deut. 24:1–4; as noted in Matt. 19:3–8).

T. W. Manson saw the two basic characteristics of Jesus' use of the Old Testament in (1) his profound insight into the essential teaching of the Scriptures; and (2) his sure judgment of his own contemporary situation.[50] It is his conviction that this approach should provide "the standard and pattern" for our own exegesis of the Scriptures. To this problem we shall return later.

Sensus literalis and sensus plenior

B. Childs has noted that the thrust of early church and medieval interpretation was to emphasize the multiple layers of meaning *above* the text, while the thrust of the modern period was the multiple layers *below* the text (that is, the historical setting, the process of handling the tradition, which leads on to canonization).[51] Thus in recent times the importance of the literal sense of the text has been reduced, and the present has been separated from the past.

He argues for the importance of retaining the reality and the inspiration of the text, for it (with its content) is the proper object of biblical research. Because the text must be studied in relation to the community of faith, the literal sense and the canon belong together. It is the literal sense which is the basis for moving the text into the present, and text and tradition form an integral unity as the living Word of God. Finally, it is the role of the Holy Spirit to effect proper actualization of the subject matter of the text for generations to come.

A widely accepted definition of both the literal sense and the *sensus plenior* ("the fuller sense") has been given by R. E. Brown.[52] The literal sense of Scripture is "that meaning which by the rules of historico-critical exegesis we can determine as the author's message for his time." The *sensus plenior* is "that meaning of the text which by the normal rules of exegesis would not have been within his clear awareness or intention but which by other criteria we can determine as having been intended by God." A basic difference between them is that the former deals with concrete realities of person, thing, and event, while the latter is on the plane of the abstract values of language.

While this "fuller sense" is usually discussed in terms of the New Testament use of the Old Testament,[53] it can be found within the latter itself. Notice the use of the Exodus narratives in Isaiah, heralding "a second Exodus"; or the apocryphal Book of Wisdom (LXX), related to the Old Testament, which fully elaborates the theme of Prov. 8:22ff.; or the practice of the Qumran writers in drawing out a fuller sense of the Scriptures.

We may rightly ask if there is any "control" on this method. How does one discover the *sensus plenior*? The context of the whole Bible is important, that we might see the larger picture and be aided by "comparing Scripture with scripture." Further, one should relate the texts used in the

New Testament back into their original contexts, thus seeing the source from which they originated.[54] Again, there should be homogeneity with the literal sense and an organic connection of the two.[55]

To be sure, it is difficult to limit oneself to a purely literal sense of Scripture. There are some factors which point toward a relativizing of this approach in practice, if not in theory.[56] First, no author is ever "neutral," nor are various implications in his words ever absent. There is some truth in the response that this renders uncertain any particular interpretation of an author's words, yet it does not do away with the problem. Or to say that "God intends" only a single meaning still leaves that meaning to be found.

Second, to understand an author today is to understand differently than would another interpreter or audience. One may reply that this factor changes not the meaning of the text, but rather its significance. The meaning is represented by the author's use of certain sign-sequences; the significance is how the text relates to a person or situation.

Third, to fulfill a command in the text appropriately will involve a change in meaning from the original situation. That is, to understand a command indicates its application in a concrete situation. If the situation is new, what does the command then mean?

These observations point up once again the existing tension between what an author "meant" and what the text "means" to a reader. The complexity of the situation remains, and one ultimately must use his best judgment in trying to understand what the original sense of the text was, a task which calls for both grammatical-historical and theological exegesis.

This can be illustrated from any number of examples of texts in the Old Testament, where the question arises, is more intended than appears in the historical situation? In both Isa. 7:14 and Hos. 11:1 the reference appears to be to the sequence of events in the Old Testament history. The former relates to the situation in the day of King Ahaz, when he was threatened by the Syro-Ephraimite coalition. The child "Immanuel," soon to be born, would be God's sign of deliverance for Ahaz and his nation. Yet notice both indications within the context (Isa. 9:6–7, "unto us a child is born") and the use of the text in Matt. 1:23. Do we then refer to "multiple fulfillment" or *sensus plenior* in reference to Isaiah's words?

The same is true in Hos. 11:1. The text appears to refer back to the Exodus event, to the experience of the nation. Yet Matthew's use of the text (2:15), based on the principle of corporate solidarity, shows that which applies to the nation has been focused on Christ. So we ask, did God "intend" these later fulfillments of the texts in the life of Christ? Was that inherent in the original prophecies?[57]

Some Old Testament passages seem to imply a deeper meaning within themselves.[58] For example, Isaiah 53 expresses the need for redemption and assures that God would bring it about (vv. 4–6, 10). Yet the solution lay beyond the Old Testament. Or in 2 Samuel 7, a successor to David is promised which seems to lie beyond the days of Solomon and his temple (notice the language of vv. 13, 16).

These kinds of texts may illustrate for us a *sensus plenior.* Yet to maintain some control in exegesis one should begin with the literal sense of the text, observe the total context, realize that the divine purpose in history is certain of fulfillment (on God's terms), and include both Old and New Testaments to have a measure for interpretation.

In conclusion, we return to the question as to whether Jesus' approach to the Old Testament should provide the standard and pattern for our own exegesis, as T. W. Manson suggested. To put the question in a wider form, we may ask it in this way, "Can we reproduce the exegesis of the New Testament?"[59] The answer must come in terms of both yes and no.

To argue that the exegesis of the Old Testament by the New is arbitrary is to overlook the factors we have noted, primarily the awareness of context and the Christological focus of exegesis. To argue that our modern methods of study (whether grammatical-historical or existential) leave a gap between ourselves and the New Testament methods is to overlook the necessity that the descriptive also becomes normative in certain cases. For example, descriptive phrases or narratives may carry profound implications—if God is righteous, his people ought to be righteous; if God answered his people when they called upon him, believers today should exercise faith in and prayer to God as well; if the early believers were "all of one mind," this becomes a pattern for later generations. Further, we can affirm "a continuity of faith" between those of biblical times (the prophets and apostles) and ourselves.

R. Longenecker has given three suggestions for solving the problem of relationships:[60]

(1) There is a need for adequate understanding of the exegetical procedures found in the New Testament. This is a matter for historical, linguistic study.

(2) There is a need to appreciate the purpose of biblical revelation. Why has God revealed himself in Scripture? This is a theological issue.

(3) There is a need to develop an awareness for what is descriptive and what is normative in the biblical revelation.

Having said this he acknowledges that a major issue remains, for we cannot reproduce their *pesher* exegesis that is founded upon a revelatory stance; or their exegesis which was circumstantial in nature (for example, Paul's use of "seed" in Gal. 3:16). Also, to know whether certain texts are purely descriptive or also normative is often difficult. In any number of cases, Jesus and the apostles were unique in their methods (John 15:27; Eph. 2:20; Rev. 21:14); in addition, much of the "Jewish manner of argumentation" should not be attempted, as it is part of the cultural context for a transcultural, eternal gospel. This is mainly to say that the New Testament is not a textbook on the science of hermeneutics.

What is left for us then? Primarily we must make use of a literal, grammatical-historical method of exegesis in following the apostolic faith and doctrine. A combination of historical and theological insights is the way we can best approach the biblical text in a manner that is in keeping with the intent of Scripture and that will render the text a rule for faith and practice.

CHAPTER FIVE

Interpretation in the Church

"THE PRINCIPLE OF inspiration points up in hermeneutical fashion... that scripture cannot be understood in isolation from the referent and experience of the church and a lived faith."[1]

As we have seen in earlier remarks, the interpretation of the Old Testament in the New involved a critical use of the Scriptures. Jesus and the apostles used the sacred writings in ways which show both their awareness of distinctions in the historical settings and later applications made possible by the Holy Spirit speaking to the people of God.

Early Church Fathers

"The exegesis of the primitive Christian Church was a direct and unself-conscious continuation of the type of exegesis practiced by ancient Judaism in its later period."[2] This, which had been true of the apostolic period, continued on well into the second century and beyond, when it was joined by Christian exegesis of the New Testament as well. There was use of "cautious allegory" and a developed typology, seen especially in Melito of Sardis and Justin Martyr.

Much of the early exegesis depended on the writer's view of the Old Testament, particularly in relation to the New Age. Here are some examples from late first and second century books:

(1) 1 Clement took the scarlet thread of Rahab's house (Josh. 2:18) to foreshadow that "all who believe and hope on

God shall have redemption through the blood of the Lord" (12:7); and see 42:5 on Isa. 60:17.

(2) The Epistle of Barnabas attempted to allegorize the food laws of the Jews and apply them to the life of the Church. To "eat of every animal that is cloven hoofed and ruminant" (Lev. 11:3) means that "the righteous both walks in this world and looks forward to the holy age," and also meditates on the word of the Lord (10:11). A very curious interpretation is given to the 318 men of Abraham's household. In Greek this number is expressed by three letters: TIH. In the IH (= 18), he claims we see Jesus (for IH, in Greek, are the first two letters of Jesus' name); in the T (= 300), there is the Cross through which the grace of Jesus comes to us. He ends with the word, "No one has heard a more excellent lesson from me, but I know that you are worthy" (9:8–9).

(3) Melito of Sardis, in his Paschal Homily 59, considered Abel, Isaac, Joseph, Moses, David, and the prophets as types of Christ:

> Accordingly, if you desire to see the mystery of the Lord, pay close attention to Abel who likewise was put to death, to Isaac who likewise was bound hand and foot, to Joseph who likewise was sold, to Moses who likewise was exposed, to David who likewise was hunted down, to the prophets who likewise suffered because they were the Lord's anointed.

(4) Justin Martyr, in his Dialogue 54, takes "the blood of grapes" (Gen. 49:11) to signify the blood of Christ; and in Dialogue 61 we find the first occasion of a Christological interpretation of the words of Prov. 8:21–31.

But there was much variety within church interpreters in the second century. Among them are the so-called heretics— those who did not share the view that the Old Testament as well as some of the New Testament books, was Scripture (see 2 Pet. 3:16). One of these was Marcion of Pontus, a representative of one of many "Gnostic" interpreters. The Gnostics apparently began the allegorization of the New Testament,[3] while Marcion himself rejected the entire Old Testament as unworthy (from a philosophical-theological viewpoint). From the standpoint of a dualism, Marcion saw two gods: the Creator and God of the Law, and the good God, Father of Jesus Christ. He rejected the Old Testament and the Gospels (except for a shortened version of Luke), and gave special place to Romans and Galatians. His interpretation of Scripture tended to be quite literal, and he strongly opposed the allegorical method. Many of his followers and other Gnostics, however, did engage in the use of allegory. For example, the five "foolish virgins" in Jesus' parable (Matt. 25:1ff.) were taken by some to represent the five (deceptive) senses.

It was Tertullian of the Latin church who charged that "allegories, parables, and riddles" characterized the Gnostic interpretation of the New Testament. The response of the Church was to produce their own allegory. While Tertullian himself used allegory with a degree of restraint, it was used in the Alexandrian church, following the example of the first century Jewish scholar Philo.

Philo was a Jew of Alexandria, but he drew heavily upon the methodology of the Greeks, who had interpreted the writings of Homer and the Greek mythologies. Passages in these writings which attributed unseemly actions to the gods, or which were otherwise offensive, were allegorized to bring them into accord with current philosophical or moral ideas. Philo had also seen in the Stoic writers a twofold approach to allegorizing: the "physical" and the "ethical." The former Philo used to interpret Scriptures relating to God and the world; the latter to those relating to the duties of mankind.[4] Abraham, for example, represented the soul on its journey, first encountering the realm of the senses, represented by Hagar, but then rising to the level of true wisdom, represented by Sarah.

Generally anything in the Scriptures deemed unworthy of God must be allegorized. This applied as well to elements that were difficult to understand. Philo found beyond the literal sense several levels of deeper meaning, and his approach was distinctly anti-historical. Commenting on Manasseh and Ephraim, the two sons of Joseph, he wrote: "Fitly is he younger, for his name means 'from forgetfulness,' and that is a thing equivalent to 'recalling to mind.' But the first prize goes to Memory, the second to Recollection, and Ephraim is named after Memory, for his name when translated is 'Fruit-bearing,' and the fairest and most nourishing fruit of the soul is remembering with no forgetfulness."[5]

Philo's allegorical method was taken up by Clement of Alexandria, the first among Christian writers to justify and explain the meaning of this approach to the Scriptures. Clement discerned five possible senses for the words of any text:[6] (1) historical—ordinary sense of stories; (2) doctrinal—moral, religious and theological sense of statements; (3) prophetic—prophecies and "types" found in the Old Testament, (4) philosophical—as in Philo, the physical (cosmic) and ethical (or psychological) sense; and (5) mystical—a symbolic sense; for example, Lot's wife symbolizes attachment to earthly things, producing blindness toward God's truth. The key to interpretation of Scripture is Christ, for he gives the Christian knowledge to understand all of Scripture. Thus in Clement we see the allegorical method, formerly employed by Philo, now "baptized into Christ."[7]

This system was codified and developed by Origen, Clement's successor in Alexandria. His importance for the history of interpretation partially lies in raising the academic level of interpretation of Scripture. There developed a methodical, almost scientific approach to scholarship.[8]

In all of this early development we may sense some dismay, especially in light of modern attitudes toward allegorical or other non-literal methodologies in exegesis. Yet, on the one hand, the early Fathers did retain the "framework" of the Biblical message—creation, the election of Israel, the Incarnation, the Atonement, Resurrection, and Judgment. Their aim in handling Scripture was "to discover, and to preach and teach, the burden, the purport, the drift, the central message of the Bible"[9]—an aim explicitly enunciated by such writers as Irenaeus, Tertullian, and Athanasius. Apart from problems with many details, in the end result they were usually on target.

When we turn to the "rival" schools of thought at Antioch in Syria, the approach to interpreting the Bible differs markedly from that at Alexandria. Due to a greater influence from the Jewish community in Antioch,[10] the allegorical method was generally subdued by an emphasis on a more literal understanding of the Jewish Scriptures. Paul of Samosata looked for common ground between Jewish beliefs and essential Christian teachings. Lucian of Antioch and Dorotheus were students of the Hebrew text. Synagogue worship held an appeal for many Christians in Antioch, and Easter was celebrated as a Passover. The great John Chrysostom asked, "Is not the difference between us and the Jews slight? Do not the subjects of disagreement between us seem trivial? (*Adversus Judaeos* IV. 3).

The reality of biblical history, through which God revealed himself, was championed by the school of Antioch. Their interpretation was based on the letter, and this was always a base for deeper meanings. Both levels of meaning were already present in the text. To interpret Isa. 7:14 with regard to the coming of Jesus Christ was not to add a meaning to the historical sense. Both were foreseen by the prophet as he wrote.

Along with the literal sense came the use of typology. Lucian of Antioch (A.D. 240–312), founder of the Antiochean school, propounded two rules: (1) Every passage has a literal meaning and only one; (2) along with the literal sense is the typological (showing the relation between the old and new covenants).

Theodore of Mopsuestia, John Chrysostom, and Jerome were the leading exegetes and commentators of Antioch. Among them they show something of the variety present within this school.[11] Theodore was the most literalistic; Chrysostom stressed the typological method (as giving "the final form of the portrait"); and Jerome gradually moved more and more toward an emphasis on the historical reality of the Old Testament narratives and prophecies, which was the basis for a spiritual understanding of the text.

This literal-historical approach to exegesis would have its impact upon the later Church, although the Alexandrian influence was the stronger during most of the Middle Ages. Through Thomas Aquinas and the Reformers, the literal-historical method survived to become the primary approach to the interpretation of Scripture within the Church. Two examples will illustrate the point.[12] One must belong to the true, orthodox church, said Tertullian, and adhere to "the rule of faith" held dear by the Church in order to give a true exposition of Scripture. This "rule of faith" was regarded as that proclaimed and taught in the writings of the New Testament. Thus the many individual interpretations would be tested.

Similarly, Augustine emphasized the kind of interpretation which reflected the rule of faith. He laid down certain requirements for the task of interpretation: (1) determine the true text of Scripture, and a clear concept of the inspired canon, (2) gain a knowledge of Hebrew and Greek (the original languages of the Bible) and, (3) a capacity for distinguishing the literal and the derived sense of Scripture.[13] A kind of practical test was added by Augustine. Purity of life and soundness of doctrine should stem from a literal interpretation. Otherwise, the sense of the word is figurative. Love of God and one's neighbor is what is meant by purity of life; and, knowledge of God and one's neighbor is the meaning of soundness of doctrine.

The Middle Ages

This period spanning the thousand years or so from the early Fathers to the Reformation produced not as many striking, innovative developments, as it did produce transitional aspects of interpretation.[14] Exegesis was separate from theology, the latter being largely joined to philosophy, and the philosophical framework moved from a Platonic to an Aristotelian plane. Both these movements may be seen in the work of the thirteenth century scholar Thomas Aquinas. The allegorical method was predominant (although its opposite was not lost, as can be seen in the work of Andrew of St. Victor), propounded throughout the Middle Ages in a Latin verse describing the four senses of Scripture:

> Literal shows us what God and our fathers did;
> Allegorical where our faith is hid;
> Moral gives us rules of daily life;
> Anagogical shows us where we end our strife.

A standard illustration of the breadth of this exegesis is the comment on the meaning of the name "Jerusalem" in Gal. 4:25f.: (1) historically means the city of the Jews; (2) allegorically means the church of Christ; (3) morally means the human soul; and (4) anagogically means the heavenly city, mother of us all.

While these four senses were not exclusive, they tend to be representative. For some, as Gregory the Great (sixth to seventh century A.D.), the *sensus spiritalis* and particularly the *sensus moralis* were of such importance that the literal sense was nearly eliminated.[15] This can be seen in Gregory's exposition of the book of Job.

Why this continued use of multiple senses? First, there had not been any adequate explanation of the relation of revelation to reason. In view of the lack of a satisfactory natural theology, as much as possible had to be drawn from Scripture. Second, through the influence of Platonism, it was widely held that God's words and will were hidden in Scripture and had to be discovered. The language of the Bible, then, was primarily symbolic.

Toward the end of this period, the influence of Aristotle's philosophy became stronger, and a greater rationalism was in keeping with a more literal exegesis. Thus the allegorical method began to decline. This new approach (or revival) is seen especially in Thomas Aquinas. Thomas asserted that the "first signification whereby words signify things belongs to the first sense, the historical or the literal." The spiritual sense is based on the literal and presupposes it. He allowed also for the allegorical, moral and anagogical senses, for "it is not unfitting . . . if even according to the literal sense one word in holy scripture should have several senses." (Not several *literal* senses but apparently several senses built upon the literal.)

So the movement to bring exegesis and theology back together was illustrated in Thomas' expositions, an emphasis that would surface in the Reformation. Along with Aquinas could be mentioned Nicholas of Lyra,[16] who also posited the literal sense as a base for other senses. It has been said, "If Lyra had not piped, Luther would not have danced."

Reformation exegesis

Lorenzo Valla, in the fifteenth century, was a key link between the Renaissance and the Reformation. From his work in textual criticism, it was clear that Scripture ought to be interpreted by the laws of grammar and the laws of language. This kind of direction gave birth to historical exegesis of Scripture in the new era. And the work of the Reformers gave rise to exegeting the Bible as the Word of God—a Book speaking to the deepest needs of humanity.

Martin Luther, reared in the use of the allegorical method, showed a great change following his conversion. After 1517 he set aside allegorizing, saying that "only a single, proper original sense makes good theologians," and that to allegorize is "to juggle with Scripture."

John Calvin practiced a grammatical-historical interpretation. This comes out clearly in his many commentaries on Scripture, for he was first an exegete, then a theologian. F. W. Farrar states "the most characteristic and original feature of his Commentaries is his anticipation of modern criticism in his views about the Messianic prophecies."[17]

The Reformers retained both Scripture and the Church's

consciousness of faith, but reversed the balance held pre-
viously—that is, decisive weight was given to the former not
the latter. It is only from Scripture, they insisted, that we
hear the gospel concerning the mission, death, and resurrection of Christ. And Scripture must be understood only
through the Spirit (encountered by us in reading the text).
Basic to their work were the priciples: *solus Christus, sola
Scriptura,* and *sola fide* (only faith).[18] These were worked
out in the threefold purpose for the exegesis of Scripture: (1)
to discover the original meaning of Scripture (it is opposed
to allegory); (2) to distinguish law and gospel (the outward
and inner meaning of Scripture, respectively); and (3) to
facilitate the preaching of the gospel.

There appears to be a significant difference between Luther
and Calvin in respect to the type of interpretation.[19] Luther
stressed the Christological test—whether a book "urges Christ
or not." Thus books like Romans and Galatians contain the
"truest gospel," and it is sufficiently clear for all to understand.
Calvin, on the other hand stressed Scripture itself as the
authority rather than a Christo-centric interpretation. Thus
Luther's approach was more "subjective"; Calvin's more
"objective."

Post-Reformation exegesis

With the emphasis in the Reformation upon the authority
of the Bible above the authority of the Church, from about
1600 onward the study of Scripture was cut free from the
supervision of the Church. Further, with the rise of the
historical-critical method of interpretation that joined with
the movement of the divine Spirit, the principle emerged that
no special or exclusive methodology was needed for theological study. Thus the interpreter could enter into the "objective"
study of the text, free from prejudice and able to share the
life and thought of his historical counterpart—the biblical
author. (The idea of "objective" study has become today a
matter of great debate among both philosophers and

theologians.) A third but negative development in this period was a growing denial that Scripture was inspired both as to content and wording. Such a belief, it was argued, did not allow for historical investigation or theological evaluation.

One of the more positive elements in this period was the work of J. A. Ernesti (see chapter one), who was perhaps, writes Farrar, the first scholar to formulate "with perfect clearness" the principle that one must determine the verbal sense of Scripture according to the same procedure used for other books.[20] This principle extends down to the present day, standing in opposition to an allegorizing, spiritualizing, or even a dogmatic approach to interpretation.

It was during this period that a great deal of skepticism regarding ancient literature arose, much of it stemming from the work of the Renaissance scholars. This attitude was applied to the Bible as well. R. M. Grant cites T. Hobbes and B. Spinoza as two examples of this literary and philosophic trend.[21] Hobbes anticipated the idea that the Bible is a record of revelation, not a revelation as such, and stressed the importance of the canon chosen by the Church, thus minimizing the authority of Scripture. Spinoza, a Jewish philosopher, championed "the absolute freedom of the human reason, released from the claims of theology."

Nineteenth century exegesis

As a radical criticism of the Scriptures had developed in the post-Reformation era, it "reached its full tide in the nineteenth century."[22] The moral philosophy of I. Kant, the historical idealism of G. Hegel, and the psychological exegesis of F. Schleiermacher contributed a new approach both to exegesis and theology. B. Ramm has given an outline summary of the characteristics of nineteenth century liberalism.[23] The following are adapted:

(1) The "Modern mentality" (Grant calls it, "philosophic presuppositions"[24]) is to govern one's approach to Scripture. This mentality had grown out of the Enlightenment of the

seventeenth and eighteenth centuries,[25] a period of great advance in learning, characterized by emphases on new attitudes toward science, history, literature, and philosophy. Man, indeed, had become the measure of all things.

(2) Both supernatural inspiration of the Bible and the miraculous within the realm of nature were rejected. Thus the theological content of the Bible was not binding; nor was one obliged to accept the occurrence of miracles as an invasion of the natural order.

(3) The religion and the sacred books of the Hebrews were the product of an evolutionary development, growing from "primitive and childlike origins." The same principle was applied to the New Testament, to the life of Jesus and the doctrines of the early Church. Because the theological content of the Bible was an accommodation to the age in which it was written, it is no longer binding.

(4) The view that the Bible was the product of various social conditions in history meant that it was "conditioned" and not able to be "canonized" (in the sense of being normative). Both predictive prophecy and typology in the Old Testament were rejected.

(5) The impact of philosophic systems on the study of Scripture and theology is seen in the moral interpretation of Scripture (as in Kant); the dialectic involving the thesis, the antithesis, and the synthesis (as in Hegel), which led to an analysis of Scripture in terms of strife and harmony; and an American ethical idealism.[26]

While much of what we have seen in summary fashion appears quite negative, there were positive developments going on at the same time. There were scholars such as C. F. Keil and F. Delitzsch, J. P. Lange, H. Alford, J. B. Lightfoot, B. F. Westcott, F. J. A. Hort, J. A. Broadus, and many others whose viewpoints and procedures were often distinct from the more liberal elements. They wrote "with genuine empathy for the basic convictions of the biblical writers who felt and declared the moving of God's Spirit in their lives."[27]

CHAPTER SIX

Interpretation Today

IN THE TWENTIETH century there is a new emphasis in the interpretation of Scripture, new at least in terms of developments and the maturity of discussion. How shall the Christian approach the Bible today? We have seen from earlier developments that the Bible ought to be read and interpreted as any other book. This approach, basic to historical criticism, has been paramount among scholars since the eighteenth and nineteenth centuries. Others have contended for at least combining historical methodology with theological presuppositions. A recent work has so voiced the concern:

> When Jesus is allowed to be interpreter of the Scriptures, a truly Christian interpretation of them, takes place. Such an interpretation takes account of the work of biblical criticism, but at the same time recognizes the need to understand the relevance of the Bible for the present day in the light of the Christian faith.[1]

Recent trends

It is possible to begin at several points when surveying recent trends in biblical interpretation. We shall look at several of the most significant areas:[2]

(1) Modern literary tools. The various literary-critical methods of recent years have moved from attempts to dig behind the biblical documents (such as in the source criticism of the synoptic Gospels or Acts), to application of hermeneutical principles by which we may "objectively" study the Scriptures.

For some, this means going beyond historical and literary issues to the theological teachings of the Bible.

(2) The New Hermeneutic. Stemming primarily from studies in the 1960s, the basic starting point of this approach is "the common humanity and historicality of (both) the text's author and the text's interpreter." It is a way of dialoguing with the text; in the process, the interpreter finds himself subtly changed. The interpreter responds to some claim that the text is making upon him, such as a call to decision.

(3) Canon criticism and hermeneutics. As a result of the work of J. A. Sanders,[3] emphasis is laid upon the process in which the traditions, (oral or written) were re-formed to meet the needs of believing communities in Israel (Old Testament) and the Church. Thus attention is given to the contexts of the documents as well as to the texts themselves. This becomes a pattern for our use of the texts today.

(4) Structuralism. As a complex approach, structuralism affirms that "truth" derives not from the intent of the author of a text, but from "the deep structures of the human mind." It is a new form of language study (compared to the grammar and philology of the past). Both the evolution of language, and language as a living whole; both a stored vocabulary (common to a community), and a used-language; both "that which is signified," and "that which signifies"; and both a linear sequence of signs (words) in a sentence, and an associative system (in which one word suggests others like it)—these are basic elements in the system emphasizing that "language is form, not substance."[4]

(5) The Maier-Stuhlmacher Debate. This centers around the validity, even the very usefulness, of the historical-critical method of Bible study. G. Maier has called for an end to the use of this method, preferring to use what he calls a "historical-Biblical" method.[5] But the question arises, how does one define the historical-critical method? Does it necessarily mean the interpreter claims to stand in judgment over the Word of God? Can it not be used as a tool apart from such presuppositions?

One may ask, after even such a brief description, is there a superior method among biblical methods? We must answer that exclusive rights of approaching the biblical text cannot be claimed by any one method. Further, good tools must be used knowledgeably to bring one to a better understanding of and obedience to the Word of God.

Historical-critical exegesis

As we shall see, the large shift in the overall hermeneutical scene today is the shift from the text to the interpreter; the shift from the past to the present; the shift from the rationalist to the existentialist approach of reading a text. The historical-grammatical interpretation once stressed the language of the Bible itself as the primary object and focus; while the "New Hermeneutic" stresses that language in the Bible has a "performative function"; that is, it creates a new situation of faith in and submission to Christ.[6] If we put too much emphasis on the propositional nature of the Biblical revelation, we may be elevating the mind above the heart. Further, Scripture describes truth not mainly from an intellectual, but from an existential standpoint; that is, the whole self is committed to and sanctified by it (compare John 17:17).

What is meant by a "critical" method of interpretation? To be sure, many "critical scholars" do hold presuppositions antithetical to the theism of the Bible, or to the idea of revelation, or to inspiration. But the term itself is not so directed. It stems from the Greek word *kritikos*, meaning one who judges or discerns. With respect to Scripture study, criticism means "making intelligent judgments about historical, literary, textual, and philogical questions which one must face in dealing with the Bible, in the light of all the available evidence, when one recognizes that the Word of God has come to men through the words of men in given historical situations."[7] G. E. Ladd prefers the term "historical-theological criticism," as it implies two dimensions of study.[8]

Nor do all modern users of the historical-critical method accept anti-supernaturalistic presuppositions. The writings of such German scholars as W. Kummel and L. Goppelt, or the

Americans F. V. Filson and W. Brueggemann, along with many conservatives in evangelical ranks would show that to be so. An interesting debate was carried on recently between N. Cameron and I. H. Marshall, two British evangelical scholars.[9] Cameron opposes the use of the method as a hermeneutical tool due to its skepticism (which he believes is not separable from it). He uses a Christological analogy; that is, even as Christ is unique, so is Scripture. We cannot discover the deity of Christ by use of historical/human study; nor can we discover the essence of Scripture by such an approach. Marshall affirms the possibility of using a historical approach which is free from these unsatisfactory presuppositions. He grants that historical study gives "probabilities" rather than "certainties," but asks, is it not helpful to show that probabilities are in favor of what Scriptures say rather than against it? He prefers the term "grammatico-historical" exegesis.

It may be that results gained from historical exegesis are not necessarily far separated from theological or supernatural elements in the text of Scripture. It is true that Bultmann defines history in a way that sees individual events connected by the succession of cause and effect, thus comprising a closed continuum. Yet, suggests D. Fuller, causation need not be limited to what is immanental.[10] If all immanental explanations have been exhausted, a supernatural cause might be considered. Paul's conversion may stand as an example of such a phenomenon. When we see "redemptive history" woven into "ordinary history," as in the Incarnation (John 1:14), then the historical method may come into play to interpret and aid in validating the canonical literature.

There is an ordering of things in the universe brought about by the sovereign Lord. As we look at Scripture, both historical event and interpretation are to be considered within the divine ordering.[11] This perspective is part of the illuminating work of the Holy Spirit—a necessary work due to the effects of sin upon our beings. Without it the intended meaning of many biblical statements will be distorted or even missed completely in our study of Scripture.

This may mean that, as students of the Bible, we need to

broaden our understanding of revelation to include insights from sober historical study. The variety of theologies (for example, the descriptions of God in the book of Isaiah, the book of Jeremiah and the gospel of Matthew) should give an opportunity for appreciating the relation between revelation and specific historical situations. Other examples include the well-known contrast between Paul and James on the theology of justification or the relation of the books of Chronicles to those of Samuel and Kings.

Is it possible to be critically stringent in exegesis, yet be open to transcendance and dialogue with the text?[12] The question is a difficult one, and the attempt to balance this has often suffered abuse or, at least, is "the methodological equivalent of mixing oil with water." Part of the answer, the whole of which has not yet appeared, is probably to be found in one's view of history and revelation. If there is a boundary between historical and theological materials, and between two ways of understanding the Bible, some bridge must be built.

Insights from other disciplines may be helpful bridges to the biblical scholar, giving a fuller understanding of what it is we are about in sober study of the Bible. Recognizing that we do bring some frame of reference from outside the text can be the first step. We may distinguish two types of criteria for analysis: the aesthetic and the ontological.[13] Beginning with the literal meaning of the text, we ask why the story is important. The ontological criterion, on the other hand, is concerned with the truth of what is in the text. Some would see a "natural religion" within man, giving a way of measuring biblical statements. Others, of course, would appeal to the illumination by "the Spirit of truth." Yet the disciplines of psychology/psycho-analysis, sociology, or structuralism could prove useful.[14]

Other issues and approaches

One of the recent trends, listed at the beginning of this chapter, deserves a more detailed examination because of its impact. We shall sketch some of the key emphases, give examples from some of the exponents, and conclude with some discussion and criticisms.

At the outset we see emphasis on the text interpreting the reader; that is, the text of Scripture is not the object, but the principle of interpretation. So the text explains the present. Language has a divine potency about it as used in Scripture—it is an "effective event."[15] Language is a supreme expression of being, the means by which man understands himself and his world.[16] If this approach is applied to Scripture, the Word of God primarily sheds light on the whole of our existence, rather than adding a new object to our horizon of knowledge. Until I have understood myself better with the help of the Bible, I have not yet really and totally understood the Bible.[17]

It was the work of Schleiermacher that brought about the new approach in the history of interpretation, a change to a way of making understanding possible.[18] The art of such understanding can begin after the interpreter identifies with the originator/author of any discourse. (The preparation comes through historical and linguistic knowledge.) One needs to perceive how the universal (infinite) is represented in the particular (finite). In his later writings Schleiermacher favored a psychological understanding of the individual being; that is, in what sense the individual discourse or act is an aspect of the total life.

G. Ebeling begins one of his books with the sentence, "Boredom with language, boredom with words."[19] He notes that the "theology of the Word" concept, arising in Schleiermacher and others, was the result of "a vigorous apprehension of the paradox of the word of God in human language, as an impossible possibility."[20] The basic problem in the recent history of theology has been the lack of assent freely given to the tradition of Christian language. Words have become meaningless as far as our experience is concerned. What we need is "the language of faith," which is described as "the dialogue of faith with the experience of the world."[21] This will help to critically test and provide exercise for the language of faith. An understanding of language comes in the context of the knowledge of God, the knowledge of oneself, and the knowledge of the world.[22]

All of this means a personal involvement in a world that seems distant, the world of the biblical authors. One must place himself in the author's milieu. We attempt to understand "the basic question of all understanding"—that of individual human existence. By gaining insight into another individuality, the meaning of human existence is disclosed in greater depth.

Thus we are brought to "the fundamental hermeneutical problem of the temporal distance between interpreter and author."[23] Can this distance be overcome through historical and linguistic research; through viewing "a typical human being"; through self-understanding? Can these universals provide a principle for understanding every individual phenomenon?

H-G. Gadamer appeals to the understanding that comes by experience—usually the experience of "being pulled up short by the text."[24] Either it means nothing to us or something different than we expected. We need to see that we are part of history, and our prejudices constitute part of "the historical reality" of our being.[25] This limitation is our "horizon"—what we see from our particular vantage point. Thus to be delivered from this situation means to achieve "the right horizon of enquiry for the questions evoked by the encounter with tradition."[26]

A summary of the major motifs of the "New Hermeneutic" could include:[27]

(1) Through "word" or "language-event" our genuine being or authentic existence is being expressed. Words show reality; they "let us be seen." "Out of the fulness of the heart a man speaks" (Matt. 12:34).

(2) The language-event is the occasion of revelation. Here the "mystery of being" (God) is encountered. In the historical event of the Incarnation God came to expression, and in Jesus' life we see best the answer to the question, "Who are you?"—a message to be proclaimed anew by the Church.

(3) The spoken word is powerful (as we see in the Old Testament prophets). It brings change into life. As language reaches out, love is manifested.

(4) To speak of God and man is an attempt to understand the reality man experiences through language. Thus "theology is anthropology." In this light we attempt to understand ourselves and our fellow human beings.

As we see also in the Reformers, their emphasis on Scripture calling for the hearer to answer by faith and confession is existential in nature. "We are grasped by Christ in the Word, rather than ourselves grasping the Word historically or as a quarry for scholastic argument."[28] The question, thus, is brought before us again—how do we reconcile the rational presuppositions of exegesis with the revelationary, dogmatic basis of faith? Or to put it in other terms, of what does a proper "theo-hermeneutical" approach consist?

In dealing with a "Christian understanding" of Christian Scripture and the tradition of the Church, the following basic ingredients are suggested:[29] (a) an education in human existence—to realize that concepts such as "gratitude" or "joy" indicate certain capacities; these are divine gifts, not human achievements; (b) certain objective truths (for example, creation, incarnation, and resurrection) must be realized as part of the Christian life as such; (c) integrity, durability, and discipline in approaching the text; (d) certain directives in the task; for example, the interpreter's disposition (such as faith, prayer, and humility); the proper context for interpretation (such as respect for tradition or the rule of faith); and effective ways of listening to the text (as "the Word of God" or as prophetic words). The principal aim of a Christian understanding is the knowledge of God—knowledge not "about" but "of" God. A personal awareness of God largely determines the quality of our own being.

Evaluation

One of the leading analysts and sensitive critics of the "New Hermeneutic" is A. Thiselton. His book *The Two*

Horizons (Eerdmans, 1980) is the most thorough analysis to date. He recognizes that the basic concern in this system of interpretation is to describe how the language of Scripture may strike home to the modern reader. In what sense is it a living word which is heard anew? Here are his conclusions after a study of this hermeneutical program.[30] Undoubtedly the present danger for many is to neglect the positive insights of the "New Hermeneutic," rather than carrying the methodology too far.

(1) There is a greater concern about deep and creative understanding of the text of Scripture, and less about how one may understand it correctly. He asks whether one cannot both listen to the text as subject and alongside this critically test one's understanding of it? We cannot afford to do away with conceptualized thinking in the interest of "wholeness"; the Christian needs to use his mind to discern between what is true and what is not.

(2) There is a one-sidedness in the use of the New Testament and in relation to the message of the New Testament. (Interestingly, relatively little use is made of the Old Testament.) The new approach has given more attention to the sections using language categories such as poems, hymns, parables, etc. (as 1 Corinthians 13; the parables of Jesus) and less to the cognitive parts of the New Testament, where such forms as theological discourse or reasoned argument occur. Another factor here is that much of the New Testament is addressed to believers. In Jesus' call for decision regarding the kingdom of God, his words appear to have been often to unbelievers. So the analysis of the documents is often concerned with an attempt to get behind the tradition of the primitive church (to get at the "true" meaning).

(3) There is also a one-sided view of language in this hermeneutic. Language is not "reality" or Being itself; rather it functions on the basis of convention. The rules or conventions accepted by the language community determines effective language-activity. Also, language is not one-sidedly imperatival, conative or directive; it contains meaning, describes, and informs.

(4) This hermeneutic gives the impression of being overly-subjective; it changes theology into anthropology. One may thus become preoccupied with self-understanding. The intent, it may well be, is to give not only insight into human existence but into one's way of reacting to life, to reality, or to God.

From the standpoint of a theological exegesis of Scripture, some further issues have been raised.[31] If one grants that the biblical authors wrote in such a way as to express faith and nourish faith, then the "literal sense" of the text includes primarily theological material in the form of proclamation. This theological approach to the text served to show the common concerns and needs of the human community—how all were related to God and to each other. Is the ground of theological exegesis somehow in the text; that is, in the message of the author? If so, the "literal sense" ought to reflect what God intended to be said. This allows for a fulness of meaning. We learn from the "New Hermeneutic" that the text does not so much contain meaning, as it mediates meaning. So one may not ask, of Luke 15:3–7, "What did Luke intend to say?" but should ask, "What does the text mean?" with regard to the one lost sheep over against the ninety-nine.

The basic problem to be faced here is apropos to any scientific control of exegesis. Is it open to any interpretation? What is the criterion of validity in exegesis? It tends to appear more as an art than a science. Yet it does show possibilities for an "ordinary" interpretation of the text of Scripture.

Finally, as to an awareness of the historical dimension of Scripture and the developments of the literature, we have this evaluation.[32] The diversity of Scripture, showing God addressing many different people in different situations, is "the natural result of the one true God's graciously relating to humans, drawing humans into a relationship inviting free response and full engagement."

(5) Above all, there is concern with the "rights" of the text as opposed to the interpreter's interjection of concepts onto

the text. (In itself, the point is well taken. The Greek myth of Procrustes' Bed is re-enacted again and again by interpreters in relation to the text.) Both "content" and "experience" aspects are needed in interpretation.

In modern hermeneutics, several emphases have surfaced, relating to (a) the dimension of subjectivity (where the interpreter essentially "re-creates" a text); (b) the profound significance of language in understanding reality (where language prods us to look at life more deeply); and (c) the merging of horizons (where there is a positive role for the subjective element). Responding to each of these in turn, the following evaluations can be made:

(a) Biblical confessions are rooted in history, in real events, even while we realize that human language is the vehicle of the message that has come down to us. Both aspects need to be balanced. There needs to be a blend of events and interpretation.

(b) Divine revelation is in the patterns of order and purpose in nature and history, not through language alone. Along with "word events" there is much other material in various creation accounts, divine acts of deliverance and judgment, and eschatological expectation.

(c) The various streams of tradition giving various interpretations of events and God's role looks away from a "single horizon" which can be merged with a contemporary understanding. Biblical tradition is marked by complexity; for example, a "history-of-salvation" motif; a "royal covenant" motif; a "wisdom" motif, etc. What the past does is to give models for faithful responses to the divine activity. The new age can be seen as a part of God's ongoing activity, "an age-long trajectory" of divine works.

To conclude, we see that there is more to language as a human activity; there is more to the "language-event" as a medium of insight. It is based upon the divine gift of a Creator who is described in Scripture as "a speaking God." Writers of various persuasions stress this point, based as it is on biblical statements (Heb. 1:1; 12:25ff.). Both the writers of Scripture and the Church through the ages speak because God has first spoken.[33]

As we approach the text, with whatever pre-understanding we bring to it, we need to be aware of both concepts *and* cognitive interests that we bring.[34] There are conceptual elements such as "history," "revelation," or "miracle." They are basic to what we do in interpreting. We bring also concepts like "knowledge," "God," "man," or "the world." In addition, there are cognitive interests; for example, a practical concern which leads us to acquire knowledge. To what do we intend to apply our discoveries? These organize our experience of reality and, in that sense, are a limiting factor in our exegesis. This should be recognized for its practical value in dealing with what appear to be disagreements about the meaning of the text.

CHAPTER SEVEN

Language: Its Meaning and Use

SAINT AUGUSTINE COMMENTED as follows on the task of interpreting Scripture: "There are two things on which all interpretation of Scripture depends: the mode of ascertaining the proper meaning, and the mode of making known the meaning when it is ascertained."[1] Likewise, with special reference to the Old Testament, D. N. Freedman requires a "respectful approach to the Bible," consisting of two elements: (1) a respect for "the plain meaning of the text" and for what the author/speaker intended to communicate; and (2) respect for the biblical tradition; that is, the pattern of religion and history belonging to Israel found in it.[2]

As we read, interpret and apply the teachings of the Bible, we engage in a task similar to that involved in reading any book or document. This is the point that is made in contemporary hermeneutics, for example, when reading the parables of Jesus. Important to our work, however, is a special point: the Bible claims to be the Word of God, thus calling for our unique personal response.

We may notice the many instances in the Bible where the writer wishes to impress the "Word of God" character of the message upon the reader. The words which Joshua recorded in "the book of the law of God" were regarded as "the words of the Lord which he spoke to us" (Josh. 24:26, 27). Again and again Jeremiah refers to "the word of the Lord" coming to him, a way of emphasizing that his message was God's word (1:1, 2, 4). He had stood in "the council of the Lord (23:18, 22; compare Isa. 6:1–7; 40:1–2). The Bible is authoritative because it is God's Word, and not the least part of it is to be discarded, disregarded, or altered (Matt. 5:17–19; Rev. 22:18–19).

If we would grasp the language of a spoken message or a document, we must first know the meaning of the words contained therein. Words are the units of thought as they come together in sentences. We can investigate the etymology of words (how they are formed from their various elements), compare them (how they are used in various contexts), and observe their cultural aspects (available to us in Bible dictionaries, word-study books, and commentaries).[3]

The starting point for interpretation is to discover the primary significance of a word, to see how it is used in any particular case, and what shades of meaning it has acquired in its history. Words have certain grammatical forms (nouns, verbs, adjectives, prepositions, etc.). They are linked together in certain ways, which is called syntax; namely, "the arrangement of words (in their appropriate forms) by which their connexion and relation in a sentence are shown" (*Oxford English Dictionary*, Vol. X).

Interpreters have referred to "the grammatico-historical sense" of words, meaning the sense required by the laws of grammar and the facts of history.[4] This is essentially what we mean by the "literal" sense. It is based on the belief that the writers of the Bible used the current language of their location and time (the *usus loquendi*) based on the laws or principles of universal grammar, making communication possible everywhere. The study proceeds on the belief that the author's usage is primary, and that his words and sentences have one meaning in any particular instance, a meaning to be discerned from its context. Granted, the literary forms will vary since the author may use poetry or prose, narrative or letter, didactic or hortatory form, etc. (This aspect will be taken up in the chapter to follow, "Literary Forms in the Bible.")

This approach stands in contrast to one we have discussed earlier (chapters one and six); namely, that the standpoint of the reader is the crucial issue. "Meaning" we see in what the author wrote and intended (judging from his language); "significance" is what it means to the reader but is based upon the author's meaning. Once the text has been written, an author has committed himself. Any change in meaning will necessitate a rewriting of the text.

W. C. Kaiser, Jr. has stressed that the principles of interpretation be properly grounded.[5] He elaborates the following rules:

(1) The Bible should be interpreted in the same manner and with the same principles as one uses with all other books. (He notes "the manner" appropriate before the 1946 "literary revolution.") As God has revealed himself in our language, so we study the ordinary rules of language.

2) The general principles of interpreting are native to human beings as creatures created in the image of God. Humanity was given and has practiced the gift of communication and speech. To acquaint ourselves as hearers/readers with what the speaker/writer is attempting to communicate, is an art to be developed.

(3) The act of receiving and applying what an author says is distinct and secondary to the primary act of understanding his language. To refer to "significance" of language is to say that there is a relationship between the author and some person, idea, or situation. The two ought not to be confused.

In a study of the language of Scripture, certain elements are of key importance. We must consider: (a) the text of the Bible; (b) the meaning of words, beginning with etymology and the history of usage; then (c) grammar and syntax; and (d) the importance of context.

The text of the Bible

Before interpreting a text, one must be assured of the accuracy of the text. Is this what the author originally wrote? While most readers may not have a knowledge of Hebrew and/or Greek to be able to read the Bible in its original languages, they can be assured that the science of textual criticism has provided readers with a highly accurate reproduction of the original text. Despite many variants in the original language texts, scholars assure us that our present editions of the Bible, along with several good English translations, give a sound basis for proceeding to interpretation of the text.[6] In any particular passage, consulting a critical-text commentary may be a help to discover what possible readings of the text we need to be aware of.

Etymology and the history of usage

The possible dangers of depending too heavily on this aspect of word-meaning has been pointed out by J. Barr.[7] Etymology "studies the past of a word, but understands that the past of a word is no infallible guide to its present meaning... such value has to be determined from the current usage and not from the derivation." He cites the frequently-used illustration of the English "nice" being derived from Latin *nescius* ("ignorant"). We could add the Greek term *ekklesia* which moved from reference to people as "a called-out (group)" to a place where the "called-out" met, thus in the later sense of a "church building." Even in the earlier usage there was a distinction, it appears, between the abstract, "the assembling of men," and the concrete, "the men thus assembled."[8] Further, such word-groups as "the church of the Lord" or "the church of God" go beyond the basic meaning of *ekklesia*, although for many the word "church" alone includes the additional notions. But clearly enough this is not so, as Acts 19:32, 39, 41 ("assembly") will show, for there it is a "secular" usage; that is, a gathering of Greek people, with no connection with the former usage whatever.

Take the word translated "colt" in Mark 11:2, normally taken to mean "a young donkey" in our literature (see Matt. 21:5). It is interesting to notice the description in a standard lexicon,[9] where the Greek word *polos* meant "young animal" (horse or donkey) when another animal is named in its context, but meant "horse" (not "colt") when no other animal is so found. Mark mentions one animal only: did he take it to be a "horse" (and see also Luke 19:30)? If his vocabulary was more dependent on the Old Testament than on secular Greek literature, the sense of "young donkey" would be more likely (see Zech. 9:9; Gen. 49:11).

In our concern with words, we are reminded that a word depends not on "what it is in itself, but on its relation to other words and to other sentences which form its context.[10] To lift statements out of the Bible, to divorce them from their particular situation and treat them without respect to their time-frame, will easily lead to distorting the meaning of the text.

Language is composed of interdependent terms, and the value of each results only from the simultaneous presence of others. In addition, the idea of a semantic field of terms (as opposed to particular or isolated words) is crucial to interpretation. J. Barr has illustrated the use of groups or bundles of words lying in the same semantic field.[11] This is an approach to the meaning of language "not as direct relations between one word and the referent which it indicates, but as functions of choices within the lexical stock of a given language at a given time; it is the choice, rather than the word itself, which signifies."

In a study of the words "image" and "likeness" in Gen. 1:26, we find a word group with the idea of the Hebrew word *selem* "image"—not only the term "likeness" but other terms such as appearance, shape, design, graven idol, cast idol, and statue.[12] Along with the immediate passage, one may compare Gen. 5:1 and 9:6, where the "image" terminology occurs again. Another classic section of the Old Testament is Isaiah 40–45, where similar emphases about God occur—creation, emphatic monotheism, the uniqueness of Israel's God—to give a larger thought context for understanding Genesis 1. Barr argues that one has no reason to believe the writer had in mind any definite idea about the content or location of the image of God, rather he was emphasizing that it is man who (among all creation) has a relation or an analogy to God. The word "image" itself is ambiguous; the word "likeness" is added to define and limit its meaning.

These insights are not meant to discount the *word* as a unit of meaning. It is usual that a single word has a more or less permanent meaning, a "hard core" of meaning which is, to a degree, stable. Yet its various shades of meaning should not simply be added up and brought over to any one place. For example, the Greek work *parakletos* (literally, "one called alongside") may be used as comforter, helper, advocate, or counselor in various contexts. In a specific text, such as John 14:16, what is the most appropriate rendering? Notice the following tranlations: Comforter (KJV); Helper (TEV, NKJV); Advocate (NEB); Counselor (RSV, NIV). We should not, it seems, try to read all these meanings into the single passage. Rather, we should ask, what sense best fits the context? What is the Holy Spirit in his position "alongside"?

It will be well to remember that (a) word meanings are always changing; (b) the "original" meaning does not determine later meaning(s); and (c) later meanings are discovered empirically through a study of the actual usage of a word in the various texts in which it occurs.

How, then, shall one deal with word meanings? Several principles are helpful to guide the interpreter:

(1) Become acquainted with the range of meanings of any particular word in its period of usage. For example, the English word "conversation" meant "deportment" or "behavior" in the seventeenth century, whereas in the twentieth century it refers to two or more persons "speaking together."

(2) Decide which meaning best matches the context of the writing. In 1 Pet. 3:1 the translation "conversation" (KJV) would be misleading to a twentieth century reader, for the verse states that a husband "may be won without a word" (by his wife's "behavior," rather than by her "conversation").

(3) Beware of reading modern ideas into a biblical passage by using modern psychological terms to explain Hebrew ideas such as "soul" or "self," or to read modern ideas of

economics into the parable of the laborers (Matt. 20:1–16).

(4) Lay greater emphasis upon usage than upon etymology. For example, the Greek work *koinonia* has the root idea of "sharing [in common]," and is used of "fellowship," "altruism," "a gift/contribution," or "participation." It is used of fellowship with God and with fellow-Christians; of giving money or goods to the poor; of sharing in suffering, and so on. In a particular passage, say Gal. 6:6, how would it best be understood?

(5) Beware of unwarranted distinctions between synonyms not supported by the context in which they occur. If we "read into" a text something that is not there, we substitute our own authority for the authority of the author.[13]

Synonyms are often misused by well-meaning interpreters. A synonym is "a word having the same or similar meaning as another word," and in some cases one may be substituted for the other. Yet the context in which the words occur will dictate whether or not the words are truly "synonyms." For example, are "flat" and "level" interchangeble? One may be "level-headed," but this is hardly the same as "flat-headed." Yet in other cases, "flat," "level," "horizontal," "plane," or "even" will be synonyms.

Two common terms for the idea of "word" in the New Testament are *logos* and *rhema*. Yet both words have many separate meanings. In 1 Pet. 1:25 *rhema* has the sense of the proclaimed message, the gospel, whereas in Matt. 12:36 it has the sense of a (careless) "word," and in Luke 2:15 it refers to a "thing" (an "event"). So also *logos*, meaning "the (divine) Word" in John 1:1, whereas in Heb. 13:22 it refers to the epistle, and in Eph. 6:19 it has the sense of an "utterance." On the other hand, it would appear that *logos* in 1 Pet. 1:23 and *rhema* in 1 Pet. 1:25 both refer to the proclaimed message, one "the word (of God)," the other "the word (of the Lord)," both heard in "the good news which was preached to you."

Again much discussion has been expended on the sense (or senses) of the two words for "love" (*agapaō* and *phileō*) in

John 21:15–17. Are they interchangeable or distinct? On the one hand they are closely related as containing components of affection, concern, appreciation, and the like. Some have seen the former as indicating a deeper, more profound relationship between two persons than the latter; one is "love," the other "affection." Yet notice two elements which will affect our understanding here. First, in John 21 several pairs of words occur: "haul" and "drag" (vv. 6, 8), "feed" and "tend" (vv. 15, 16), and "lambs" and "sheep" (vv. 15, 16). Possibly the basic idea is reinforced by placing these synonymous terms in close proximity; thus driving the point home.[14] Then, we see that *phileō* is always used of a love based on that relationship, while *agapaō* is a wider term which does not require that condition for its expression (that God can love sinners who are still alienated from him). Thus in our passage, where an existing relationship is in view, either term can express "love," with no difference in meaning.[15]

Grammar and syntax

The various word-forms and word-relations that occur in a text each play a role in transmitting the author's message. We need to be aware of forms such as nouns, verbs, adjectives, and adverbs, and such relations as subject, object, predicate, participle, and preposition. Grammar has to do with the structural form of words; syntax with the grammatical relations between words. While the former differs greatly with different languages, the latter is much more the same for human speech.

One must be aware of the basic characteristics of Greek and Hebrew grammar. Even for the English-only reader, these features are important, for they indicate certain senses of the language. For example, in the verb systems of the biblical languages, there is primarily a *kind* of action rather than the *time* of action. In Greek verb tenses there is either continuous, complete, or total/whole action indicated—time is confined to one verb mood, the indicative. In Hebrew the action is either complete (perfect tense) or incomplete (imperfect tense).

For an English reader, it will be well to select a fairly literal translation so as to be alerted to syntactical distinctions. Among the most helpful are the American Standard Version (1901), the Revised Standard Version (1952), the New American Standard Bible (1971), the New King James Version (1982), or C. B. Williams' New Testament (1937).

As an illustration of the Greek verb tenses, notice the verb *sozō* "to save" as used in Paul's letters: (1) *esosen* "saved," completed actions (Tit. 3:5); (2) *sesosmenoi* "have been saved," completed and persistent action (Eph. 2:8); (3) *sozomenois* "are being saved," continuous action (1 Cor. 1:18); (4) *sothesometha* "shall be saved," predictive future (Rom. 5:9, 10). In the indicative mood, the first and second examples look primarily to the past, the third to the present, and the fourth to the future.

Does syntactic structure convey meaning directly? Is the formal surface meaning what the author intended to convey? As an example, we often define the "subject" of a sentence as the "actor." Is that always so? Consider the following examples:

(1) Tom smashed the bottle with a stick.

(2) The stick smashed the bottle.

(3) The bottle smashed.

In (1) the subject (Tom) is the actor; in (2) the subject (the stick) is not the actor in the semantic sense, rather the stick must be acted upon by someone; and in (3) the subject (the bottle) cannot be the actor, for it was acted upon. We observe, then, the possibility of wide discrepancies between the *surface* meaning and the *deep* meaning. Linguists today are not agreed whether it is more particularly semantic, or that is, based on the internal structure of language.

In biblical sentences we encounter the same kind of syntactic structures. Consider the following examples:

(1) The Lord broke down Jerusalem with the Chaldean army.

(2) The Chaldean army broke down Jerusalem.

(3) Jerusalem broke down (fell to the Chaldeans).

So 2 Kin. 24:20 and 25:10 report the fate of Jerusalem, attributing it to the Lord and to the Chaldean army, respectively. According to Lam. 1:7, Jerusalem "fell into the hand of the foe." In the Old Testament the Lord is seen as the ultimate source of all things; the human (or natural) factors are looked upon as secondary, though real; while the victim ("object") is regarded as acting out a role in the drama.

A further example of syntax may be illustrated in 2 Cor. 5:14, given in two translations:

> For the love of Christ constraineth us; because we thus judge, that if one died for all, then were all dead (KJV).

> For the love of Christ controls us, because we are convinced that one has died for all; therefore all have died (RSV).

(1) The main statement is represented by the opening clause: "For the love of Christ controls us." But what does "the love of Christ" mean? Does the preposition "of" refer to *his* love for us or *our* love for him (see Gal. 2:20)? Also, the verb "controls" (*synechō*) means "to urge on, impel" someone; it is in the present tense, thus his love "keeps on" controlling us.

(2) The "if" (KJV) should not be a part of the verse; the text literally read, "that one died" for all. No question is present about the extent of the death (notice how v. 15 repeats the same thing).

(3) The death of "Christ" and the death of "all" are both described by what is called the "aorist" tense. The aorist tense described an action as a complete entity. It indicates a completed act, in both cases. Part of Paul's theology was to link these together (see Rom. 6:3–4; Col. 3:3).

(4) Christ died "for" (*hyper*) all, a word meaning "in behalf

of, for the sake of someone" (*Arndt and Gingrich*), referring to a substitutionary and a representative death (see also Eph. 5:2).[16]

A basic principle, then, of biblical interpretation is that "the sense of Scripture is to be found in the grammatical meaning of the words."[17] Through the study of the text we try to ascertain what the writer intended to convey.

The Importance of context

Context means that which is "woven together" (Latin, *contextus,* from *con-* "together" and *texere* "weave"). In a literary work, it is that which precedes and follows, being connected with the word or passage under consideration.

Attention to context is basic, for it forces the interpreter to look at the whole line of thought of the writer. The thought is usually expressed in a series of related ideas, so that the meaning of any particular element is nearly always determined by what precedes and what follows.[18]

Various contexts need to be utilized or at least considered. The reader or hearer will be aware of these and will employ them in order to select one meaning over other possible meanings. These include: (1) a *linguistic* context; either the grammar of the passage or a lexical context; (2) a *broader* context is related to the usage of the source; do the same words or concepts occur in other places in the same book or another book by the same author?; (3) the *situational* context in which the message is formulated and understood; what was the location or the event in which the word or idea was established?; (4) the *broader situational* context is related to the place, historical period, society, language, or culture involved.[19]

If one wants to understand a word in a passage, he should first determine the potential senses—what does the stock of word usage make available?—then use all available clues to select one meaning which will fit the context. In our earlier example of 2 Cor. 5:14, the immediate context (introduced by the word "therefore") appears to be the unit in 2 Cor. 5:11–21. In view of the certainty of "the judgment seat of Christ" (v. 10), Paul reverently (namely, in "the fear of the Lord") wants to persuade men to be ready for their destiny. His theme thus becomes "reconciliation" (see vv. 18–20), and the possibility of that new relationship to God is through the death of Christ (vv. 18–19). So, the "love of Christ controls us" to live for him (v. 15) as ambassadors calling men to "be reconciled to God" (v. 20).

"Context," of course, can be enlarged as one proceeds. It could include an entire book of the Bible, a group of books by the same author or several authors, the entire New Testament or Old Testament, and the Bible as a whole. Each of these contexts is proper in one way or another.

This should not be done in a mechanical fashion, however. If we appeal to a book of the Bible as context for a particular verse or other portion, it should be in the interest of discerning the character, the scope, and the basic thrust of the book. Why did Amos, Paul, or James write a particular book? What was the purpose, the occasion, or the "burden" of the author? These queries will involve us in a study of the historical setting, the circumstances, and the destination of the text. How would a study of the book of Amos as a whole unit help in interpreting the following text:

> Therefore thus I will do to you, O Israel;
> because I will do this to you,
> prepare to meet your God, O Israel! (Amos 4:12)

Or how would a study of the epistle to the Galatians as a whole aid in interpreting "a little leaven leavens the whole lump" (Gal. 5:9)?

Perhaps the idea of "contextual circles" may be a helpful figure to illustrate the connectedness of a series of related contexts. We begin with a small circle and proceed outward as the size of the contextual circles increases. Both smaller and larger circles are important to the total process, although not each one in every case. A helpful example is found in the examination of the word *elaion* "oil" in Matt. 25:1–13, where five contexts are considered:[20]

(1) The immediate context (Matt. 25:1–13). There is no direct clue in this passage itself to the meaning of the "oil." Some have taken it to be a metaphor for "being prepared for unexpected circumstances"; and yet others for the Holy Spirit, or spiritual preparedness. Yet these would be inferences taken from clues outside the text (see the following comment).

(2) The context of Matthew 23–25. This unit begins and ends with an emphasis on obedience (23:3; 25:45; compare 24:12). This could possibly suggest the idea of "good works."

(3) The context of the gospel of Matthew generally. Compare 7:13–27 and 25:1–13. Here we find an emphasis on *doing* Jesus' words (7:24), following "I never knew you" (7:23), and followed by "I do not know you" (25:12). This is a part of the "door" symbolism (7:13; 25:10), and concludes a discourse beginning with shining like lamps through good works (5:14–16). Here we move from "possibly" to "probably."

(4) The context of the New Testament generally. No further clues occur in this context.

(5) The context of the general religious environment. There is in the Jewish background a midrashic commentary on Num. 7:19, where flour mixed with oil alludes to "the Torah, the study of which must be mingled with good deeds." This would appear to confirm the conclusion noted in (3) above.

What has been done in this preceding example is to begin with a small circle (immediate context) and move out to increasingly larger circles. In so doing, one must avoid using texts in isolation; we must not work "in the flat." Each reference must be examined in terms of its context, not lifted out and joined to others as though they all had common meaning or equal weight.

CHAPTER EIGHT

Literary Forms in the Bible

UPON READING THE Bible, one soon discovers it contains different types, forms, and genres of literature. What are these various kinds and why is it important to recognize them as we read? B. Ramm has reminded us "it is necessary for the interpreter to recognize literary forms *as necessary to the interpretation of Scripture*," because the type of literary form used governs the attitude and spirit in which we approach a document. Further, "*the literary form governs the meaning of sentences.*"[1]

Is a book basically prose or poetry? Is it a story, a poem, a prophecy, or an epistle? Knowing its form will help us to discover its meaning, and also to know how to apply it to contemporary life. Is it purely objective, localized, normative, or hortatory? In other words, what is it to us? If each literary piece is a part of the Bible, which we affirm to be "the Word of God," we may ask: "How is this particular book or text the Word of God to me today?"

Consider the following samples, taken from different books of the Bible and illustrating various literary forms:

> These are the words that Moses spoke to all Israel beyond the Jordan in the wilderness (Deut. 1:1).

> After the death of Ahab, Moab rebelled against Israel (2 Kin. 1:1).

> My son, be attentive to my wisdom,
> incline your ear to my understanding;

> that you may keep discretion,
> and your lips may guard knowledge (Prov. 5:1).

> In the eight month, in the second year of Darius, the word of the Lord came to Zechariah the son of Berechiah, son of Iddo, the prophet, saying (Zech. 1:1).

> The beginning of the gospel of Jesus Christ, the Son of God (Mark 1:1).

> Paul and Timothy, servants of Christ Jesus, to all the saints in Christ Jesus who are at Philippi, with the bishops and deacons (Phil. 1:1).

> The revelation of Jesus Christ, which God gave him to show to his servants what must soon take place; and he made it known by sending his angel to his servant John (Rev. 1:1).

These samples illustrate a farewell speech,[2] a narrative history, a wisdom-poem form, a prophecy, a gospel, an epistle, and an apocalypse.

Basically we can discuss three circles, or categories, of literary genre in the Bible beginning with the largest and moving to the most detailed. There are (1) whole books of the Bible (as illustrated above); (2) major forms found usually within a larger textual unit, such as parables, allegories, and riddles; and (3) figures of speech, of a smaller dimension, such as metaphor, simile, or hyperbole.

When we apply to such language the terms "literal" and "figurative," we mean to apply it to the form of the words, not to its "referent." A statement can be said to be "literal" if it is understood in its primary, ordinary, matter-of-fact sense, whereas it can be called "figurative" when it is used in some way other than the ordinary sense. Yet a figure of speech refers to a real referent; it does convey a truth when understood in this way.

If one says, "Sharon has eaten her fill of peanut-butter sandwiches," that may well be a matter-of-fact statement. But if one says, "Sharon is fed-up with peanut-butter sandwiches," it does not refer to the state of her stomach at all, but is a figure of speech referring to the state of her mind. To say, "There is a frog in the pond" is not the same kind of statement as "I have a frog in my throat." Such expressions, sometimes called *idioms*, must be recognized in order to convey their proper message. An idiom is a form peculiar to a language and not recognizable from its grammatical construction or from the meaning of the parts that make it up.

Major literary forms or genres[3]

First, prose is the direct, plain speech of all peoples. It may be descriptive, explanatory, or emotive. One will read (a) speeches (whether proclamations or prose prayers), (b) records (various lists, laws, genealogies, letters, or rituals), and (c) historical narratives. An example of the first would be Acts 13:16–41 and 1 Kings 8:22–53; the second, Gen. 36:9–43; Ezra 7:11–26; and the third, 1 Kings. Much of the Bible reflects the use of the third category, and one of the key problems here is how to make use of this historical material; that is, how to move from the "then" to the "now." Kaiser has used the term "principlization," by which he means a way of stating "the author's propositions, arguments, narrations, and illustrations in timeless abiding truths with special focus on the application of those truths to the current needs of the Church."[4]

Second, poetry, which makes up one-third or more of the Old Testament,[5] is marked by semantic rather than syllabic parallelism.[6] Often it reflects deep emotion and burning passions; there is a marked spontaneity in it. Thus two or more lines may be employed to express the same idea, or contrasting ideas, or to build a flood of ideas. Synonymous parallelism repeats the same idea in the two lines:

> I will make men more rare than fine gold,
> and mankind than the gold of Ophir (Isa. 13:12).

It may include both a positive and a negative element within the two lines:

> Lord, all my longing is known to thee,
> my sighing is not hidden from thee (Ps. 38:9).

Antithetic parallelism states contrasting or opposing ideas in the two lines:

> They will collapse and fall;
> but we shall rise and stand upright (Ps. 20:8).

This form is common in the book of Proverbs; sometimes nearly whole chapters contain contrasting pairs of lines:

> Anxiety in a man's heart weighs him down,
> but a good word makes him glad (Prov. 12:25).

Synthetic parallelism tends to be a longer series of lines, developing an idea stated at the beginning of the series:

> The Lord is my strength and my shield;
> in him my heart trusts;
> so I am helped, and my heart exults,
> and with my song I give thanks to him (Ps. 28:7).

Third, narrative materials, while basically prose in character, make up a large part of both Old and New Testaments. Our study here may be an entire book (or books as a large unit like 1/2 Samuel and 1/2 Kings) or a story contained within a larger work. Two tendencies to be avoided in reading narrative in the Bible are a dusty, matter-of-fact exposition, and an allegorizing/spiritualizing of the details therein. A study of the historical-narrative units of Scripture must recognize the understanding of their history both on the part of Israel (OT) and the Church (NT). The history was written interpretively, giving a theological understanding, and was a witness to their faith in God. In turn, the narratives must speak to the people of God today.

This means that we must begin from the text of Scripture itself—it does not change, but we must attempt to understand what it meant to the people of that day. Then, correspondingly, it must speak again (or continue to speak).[7] The first task calls for sound principles of exegesis; the second for sensitivity to the continuing value of the text, seeing the abiding truths and values therein, applied to today's society.

Much has been written in recent years on reading the Bible as "story." One writer has described the state of the present day as one of disorientation: "We do not have a clear sense of the meaning of recent events nor a clear sense of direction for the future." But the Bible read as story has the capacity to change one's orientation and frame of reference and to form and influence a person's identity. Such a reading of narrative story shows us the character of God and the direction of his purposes.[8]

Fourth, wisdom literature appears in both Old and New Testaments—in Job, Proverbs, Ecclesiastes, Song of Solomon (?), certain of the Psalms, along with the epistle of James, and segments such as Matthew 5–7 or 1 Corinthians 2. It was known also in the intertestamental literature, such as Wisdom of Solomon and Sirach (Ecclesiasticus).[9] Within such books there are varied literary forms, the most common being the proverb, together with epic and didactic materials.

Apart from strict classification, there are two types of wisdom materials: (1) the prudential, which contain admonitions for a happy life (see Proverbs 1–9, Psalms 1 and 37, Matthew 5–7, and James), and (2) the reflective, containing a philosophical approach to the meaning and significance of life (see Ecclesiastes, and the Wisdom of Solomon, the most philosophical of all in perspective).

One of the key passages in the Old Testament is Prov. 8:22–31, for there wisdom has existed even before the creation of the world. Wisdom is personified through her assistance to the Lord in creation. For many Christian readers (since the second century A.D.), there is a relationship of some kind between Wisdom and Jesus the Logos (John 1:1–18). Probably the most noted description of the qualities of wisdom occurs in Wisdom of Solomon 7:22–23 (compare James. 3:17).

The purpose of wisdom literature was to bridge the gap between Torah ("the Law") and everyday life. It brought religion into the mundane—the marketplace of life—where one confronted practical problems. The basic message was clear: God must be central to life. Indeed, "the fear [awe, reverence] of the Lord is the beginning of wisdom" (Prov. 9:10); "Love her [wisdom] and she will guard you" (4:6).

One can interpret this kind of literature better if the cultural situation out of which it arose is understood. In the ancient Near East, including the biblical culture, the king's court and the school (teacher-pupil relationship) seem to have been the main areas. For the former, see Moses (Exod. 7:11), Daniel (Dan. 2:48) and Ahithophel (2 Sam. 16:23). Solomon was the leading figure in the Old Testament (1 Kin. 4:30, 32). For the latter, notice the frequent reference to "my son" in Proverbs (2:1; 3:1; etc.), referring most likely to a student. In intertestamental literature, the same figure appears (see Sirach 2:1; 3:1; etc.); we read the call, "Draw near to me, you who are untaught, and lodge in my school" (51:23).

Difficulties will attend the attempt to apply the maxims of wisdom universally. While they are intended to apply generally, they do not always "fit" every situation. See, for example, Prov. 12:21: "the wicked are filled with trouble," in contrast to Ps. 73:5, 12: "They [the wicked] are not in trouble as other men are . . . always at ease, they increase in riches." One might argue that the two settings were different, or that such cases are exceptions, yet difficulty in application remains.[10]

Fifth, apocalyptic literature is closely connected with prophetic writings; for some, the term prophetic-apocalyptic is preferable. By apocalyptic, we mean revelatory writings, those which claim to make known to the elect secrets long hidden. In the Bible, together with the major examples—Daniel and Revelation—some sections of Isaiah, Ezekiel, Joel, Zechariah, the Gospels and 2 Thessalonians show typical apocalyptic characteristics.

While there is no standard list of qualities, these writings are generally characterized by a contrast between this age and the age to come; visions and revelations; much symbolism (including animals, birds, angels and demons); emphasis on "the last days" and the coming of judgment, resurrection, and the life to come.[11]

This type of writing is well represented in the intertestamental period; for example, by 2 Esdras (similar in many respects to the book of Daniel), Enoch, the Assumption of Moses, along with one of the Qumran writings, "The War Scroll" (drawn from Ezekiel 38).

In interpreting apocalyptic materials great care is needed due to their unusual characteristics. Basic rules for interpreting literature still apply (dealing with history, grammar, syntax, content), yet a "literalistic" approach seems an unlikely one. The meaning of the symbols must be sought out. Often they are interpreted within the book (see Dan. 8:22ff.; Rev. 17:15–18), in another book of the Bible (Rev. 5:5 with Gen. 49:9–10), or by historical or cultural data.

As a modern illustration of the use of symbols in apocalyptic writings, here is a lively piece from the pen of Dr. F. C. Grant:[12]

> Perhaps I can illustrate these features in apocalyptic writing by a modern parallel; bringing them closer to our own times will at least make them more vivid. Soon after the end of the Second World War, I shared a "triologue" on the "Invitation to Learning" program of the Columbia Broadcasting System. The subject was "The Book of Revelation," and I tried to explain that it belonged to a literary genre, once popular, but now often literalized and hence misunderstood. In order to explain this, I read the following account of the recent war "as an ancient apocalpytist might have described it."
>
> I beheld, and lo, a great blond beast arose out of the earth, and its teeth were like the teeth of a wild boar, wherewith to tear in pieces the bodies of men; and upon its head were the horns of a wild ox, and its arms bare the seal of a cross with sharp hooks, wherewith it should card the flesh of men. And the nations trembled with fear at the sound of the armies of

this beast; and it trampled down many strongholds and cities in its raging fury. And one came on the clouds of heaven, crying, "Peace in our time"; but he bare his shield folded beneath his arm, and he said only, "Let the nations buy and sell; let the brave submit to tyranny; and let no one disturb the beast to annoy him or provoke him to wrath." And they that sat within their strong walls feared lest the beast and his armies should triumph. And after many days the beast brake down their wall wherein they trusted, and drove all before him, even to the shores of the sea. Then the God of heaven sent down a cloud and covered them, and men fled in ships to their own country. And I beheld as it were a swarm of locusts, innumerable, which the beast put forth to devour the land of the North; but a great multitude of birds appeared, and destroyed those locusts. Yet they hurt the cities where they fell, and their destruction was by few. In the night-visions I saw, and behold, another great beast rose out of the sea, and he grew greater and mightier as he drew near. And he stood upon the shore of the sea, and his armies were innumerable. Then came a great bear out of the East, and the nations rejoiced, that the great bear from the East and the strong one from the West were sworn to destroy that first beast. And they fought valiantly, and prevailed, and the name of the first beast was found no more on the earth.

Major figures of speech

To use a figure of speech is "a conscious departure from the natural or fixed laws of grammar and syntax ... [and] must be *legitimate departures* from the normal use of words for special purposes."[13] The Greeks called these forms *Schema,* and the Romans *Figura,* both meaning "a shape" or "a figure." Bullinger classifies the forms under figures involving omission, addition, and change, respectively.[14]

How can one distinguish figurative from literal speech? There are no infallible guides, for the matter often depends upon personal judgment. For example, something that is an idiom to one person may not be understood as such by another, particularly one unfamiliar with the thought forms of that culture. The following may be helpful, however, as indications: (1) if there appears to be an incongruity between a subject and a predicate—"I am the light of the world," "wisdom cries," or "trees talking;" (2) if there would result an absurdity—"I could eat a horse," "she had a narrow squeak," or "he won hands down"; (3) if the word or expression is defined within the immediate context, showing a limitation—to be "born anew" means to be "born of water and the Spirit," "he fell asleep . . . and Saul was consenting to his death," or "carried about with every wind of doctrine;" (4) if there appears to be a reason in the text for greater force, intensification of feeling, or increased emphasis ("a departure from some law, a deviation from the even course— an unlooked for change"[15]).

What is the point of using figurative language? To use words that say things more vividly and that convey meaning by their very form. Thus the message of the text is rendered more effective. Metaphors give the mind an opportunity to exercise imagination. We can quickly see likenesses between unlike things. They add imagery into statements, transforming the abstract into concrete. To refer to "fish," as does L. Hunt, with the terms "scaly, slippery, wet, swift, staring wights [creatures]," is to impart a new dimension of visualization. They add to otherwise purely informative statements an emotional intensity, thus conveying attitudes along with information. To convey the information in "I have a headache" by saying, "My head is ready to burst," is to add a dimension of emotional fervor. They concentrate much into a brief statement. To describe the nature or the extent of human life by such figures as "a dream," "like grass," or "a sign" (Ps. 90:5, 9), is to impart a multi-dimensional quality to the subject, that would otherwise take many sentences to express.[16]

In this section on "major figures" we can illustrate seven examples. Each is defined from *The Concise Oxford Dictionary of Current English*, Sixth Edition (1976).

(1) Proverb (literally "a word for/against")—a short, pithy saying in general use (for example, "better late than never").

Bullinger lists three classes of biblical proverbs:[17] (a) those quoted as already in use; (b) those, not quoted as such, very likely in use as proverbial expressions; (c) those appearing for the first time in Scripture, which have since come into general use.

One ought to look for any clues to be gained from the context of a proverb and identify any figures of speech used therein. Also, there are certain key words or themes that are common in Hebrew proverbs, such as wise/wisdom, folly, righteous, or wicked. Sometimes these characteristics or kinds of people will be identified by their attitudes toward God or fellow human beings. When proverbs appear to contradict each other, they may both be true in different circumstances (see Prov. 26:4, 5).

Following are examples from each of Bullinger's classes:

(a) "Behold, every one who uses proverbs will use this proverb about you, 'Like mother, like daughter'" (Ezek. 16:44). "It has happened to them according to the true proverb, The dog turns back to his own vomit, and the sow to her wallowing in the mire" (2 Pet. 22:22; Prov. 26:11).

(b) "The measure you give will be the measure you get" (Matt. 7:2), a proverb common in Jewish life. "It hurts you to kick against the goads" (Acts 26:14), a proverb common among the Greeks, especially.

(c) "For there is no man who does not sin" (1 Kings 8:46; compare Prov. 20:9; Eccl. 7:20; James 3:2; 1 John 1:8, 10). "It is more blessed to give than to receive" (Acts 20:35).

Proverbs are found among all peoples of the world and are expressions of "common" wisdom. They were often used to settle some issue or as proof of some argument. Because many of them arose out of concrete situations, they may or may not apply generally; others will be found to be nearly universal. In some cases proverbs are very clear; in others they are most puzzling (see the second line of Prov. 25:27).[18]

(2) Parable (literally, "to place side by side"; a comparison)— a narrative of imagined but usually real-life events, used to typify moral or spiritual relations. A parable is often an

extended simile; for example, "the kingdom of heaven is like." While there are some in the Old Testament, they are best known from Jesus' elaborate use of this figure of speech. Probably few parts of Scripture seem so difficult of interpretation (see the comments in Matt. 13:10–17), though they were meant to communicate to those ready to receive them.

Certain general principles may be helpful in studying parables, yet there are a number of exceptions:

(a) Usually parables have one main point, but not always, as there may be allegorical elements within them (see Matt. 13:18–23).

(b) A parable is not designed to "teach a moral" but to call for decision. Yet some basically instruct or inform (Mark 12:9ff.; Luke 10:37).

(c) A parable is usually true to details of daily life (farmers scattering seed, women baking bread or sweeping the house, etc.). But often the details are startling and unexpected (see Matt. 22:7; Luke 14:18; Matt. 20:9).

Basic to the modern study of parables is the emphasis on relating them (in the New Testament examples) to the ministry and message of Jesus. (The basic works of C. H. Dodd and J. Jeremias should be helpful in this regard.[19]) The theme of the kingdom of God (or, the kingdom of heaven) was central in Jesus' teaching, and it is that focus that will direct us to a most fruitful understanding of many of Jesus' parables. Some additional principles of interpretation can be given:

(d) Notice whatever context there may be for the parable; is some occasion indicated? This will not always be so; also, some parables are set within more than one context (see Matt. 18:10–14; Luke 15:1ff.).

(e) Examine the parable itself. What cultural and historical details can be identified?

(f) Determine what form the parable has; for example, instructive, polemical, hortatory, etc. Why was the parable told?

(g) Ask what main point(s) the speaker is making.

(h) See what application the parable may have to other

people and other times. Any application should proceed from the basic interpretation.

In the Old Testament the following parables may be noted, remembering that the term "parable" (Hebrew *mashal*, Greek *paroimia*) is much wider than a "story" form: Prov. 6:7–8 (related to 6:9–11); Numb. 23:7–10, 18–24 (Balaam's discourses); 2 Sam. 12:1–6 (story of two men told by Nathan to King David).

In the New Testament, there are also various forms due to the flexibility of the term "parable": Luke 4:23, while only an expression, is called a *parabole*; Luke 5:36–39, 6:39ff; Matt. 13:1–52/Mark 4:1–34/Luke 8:4–18; 13:18–19, and all major examples of the parables of Jesus.[20]

(3) Allegory (literally, "other speaking")—a picture in which meaning is symbolically represented (see John Bunyan's *Pilgrim's Progress*).

At the outset it should be noted that allegory is not the same as "allegorizing." The former is "a story put together with several points of comparison"; the latter "makes the narrative convey ideas different from those intended by the original author."[21]

Distinction between allegory and parable is often difficult due to the linguistic relationship (both stemming from the same root idea) and the easy move from parable to allegory by development of the details therein. Some see allegory as an extended metaphor. Professor Caird, after scrutinizing the relation of allegory to parable, concludes that they are "partial synonyms, and it is less important to distinguish between them than it is to distinguish between allegory, which the author intended, and allegorical embellishment or interpretation, which he did not."[22] Thus, while classification is often not without problems, the following samples may exhibit the basic qualities of allegory: Ps. 80:8–15, Isa. 5:1–6, Ezek. 13:10–16, 17:1–10, and Eccl. 12:3–7.

Some writers see no allegories at all in the New Testament (even Gal. 4:21–31!), yet there are certain passages that may be considered: John 10:1–16, 1 Cor. 3:10–15, Eph. 6:11–17, and John 15:1–10.

In the allegory at Ezekiel 13, notice how the elements are interpreted. Those who daub the wall with whitewash signify the prophets of Israel (v. 16); the rain, hail and wind signify God's wrath (vv. 13, 15); and the wall itself signifies the false hopes and delusions of the people and their prophets (vv. 15–16, 23).

The well-known allegory of the vine and the branches (John 15:1–10) shows three basic points of comparison (where one thing means another):

(a) The true vine signifies Christ (v. 1). Notice the central place of Christ in the narrative; the personal pronouns I, my, and me occur twenty-two times in ten verses.

(b) The vinedresser signifies the Father (v. 1). His work is to prune the vine (v. 2).

(c) The branches signify disciples and believers (v. 5). This factor shows a combination of factual elements with non-factual (in real life); for example, "branches" do not "act on their own," but people do. What is the point of the allegory? Possibly it is found in v. 4: keep on abiding, thus bearing fruit. A vital relationship demands a constant activity.

(4) Fable (literally, a "discourse")—a story not founded on fact, conveying a moral, especially with animals or plants as characters in the story. The usual presence of animals and plants in the fable is a way of characterizing human beings, especially their vices. Bullinger sees no fables, as such, in the Bible; others find very few. It appears that the most obvious are Jotham's fable in Judg. 9:8–15 and Jehoash's fable in 2 Kin. 14:9.[23] Both these stories convey strong condemnation of the persons against whom they were directed.[24]

Fables hold a fascination for human beings because they are "nature stories". From the ancient fables of the Greek writer Aesop to the modern fables of J. Thurber, people have enjoyed the "mirror effect" of the fable—we are really looking at our own foibles—and have had to contend with a moral that strikes home. Something like a proverb in extended fashion, the fable often deals with human pride and arrogance or gives a word of hope for the downtrodden. For the former see 2 Kings 14:10; for the latter see Ezek. 17:22–24.

(5) Riddle (literally an "opinion")—a question, statement, or description designed to test ingenuity or give amusement in discerning its meaning. A riddle is an enigmatic saying, usually intended to perplex or, sometimes, entertain. The word occurs in 1 Kings. 10:1 ("hard questions"), the wise used riddles (Prov. 1:6), the psalmist uttered "dark sayings" (Ps. 78:2), and riddles were solved "to the music of the lyre" (Ps. 49:4).

Probably the best-known riddle in the Bible is Samson's, propounded to the Philistines (Judg. 14:12–20 RSV):

> Out of the eater came forth something to eat,
> Out of the strong came something sweet (v. 14).

Samson told the riddle to stump his opponents after encountering a lion's carcase containing honey. Only when his wife revealed the secret was the riddle solved:

> What is sweeter than honey?
> What is stronger than a lion? (v. 18).

This popular riddle needs to be seen as part of a larger narrative found in Judges about Israelite-Philistine hostility. It was this condition that brought about Samson's involvement (see Judg. 14:4). Because the riddle was a part of Samson's exploits against a perennial foe, it became an important part of the tradition. By this example we see "the existential orientation of history. Samson as a one-man army is certainly exceptional. Yet the military activities of Israel…are not cold factual record. They involve human decisions, human weaknesses and failures, and human destiny."[25]

Puzzles of various kinds in the Bible have been regarded as riddles. Among them are the cryptic words "Mene, Mene, Tekel, and Parsin" (Dan. 5:25), and the mystic number "six hundred and sixty-six" (Rev. 13:18).

(6) Type (literally, "to strike, leave an impression")—a person, thing or event serving as an illustration or characteristic specimen of another thing or a class. Some basic material

has been given in the discussion of "typology" in chapter four above. Here we shall add other illustrations.

The Greek word *typos* was used of a visible impression made by a stroke or pressure; (that is, a mark or trace) of a copy, image, form, figure, or pattern.[26] In the New Testament it is used of the Tabernacle (Acts 7:44; Heb. 8:5), of the moral life (1 Tim. 4:12; 1 Pet. 5:3), and of the "types" of the Old Testament (Rom. 5:14; 1 Cor. 10:6, 11). Its counterpart is an "antitype" (1 Pet. 3:21 "baptism" and Heb. 9:24, the sanctuary "made with hands").

A type is real (person, event, or thing), as opposed to fictitious or ideal. Terry gives five different classes of types:[27] (a) Persons: Adam (see Rom. 5:14), Elijah, Abraham, Melchizedek, etc. (b) Institutions: Sabbath, Passover, etc. (c) Offices: Prophets (Deut. 18:15), Priests (Heb. 4:14), and Kings (Ps. 2:6). (d) Events: Flood, Exodus, serpent of brass, etc. (e) Actions: Moses lifting up the serpent; Jeremiah going to the potter's house (Jer. 18:1–6).

(7) Symbol (literally "to place together"; a mark or token) —something that recalls another thing having analogous qualities or that is associated with it in fact or thought ("lion" for "courage"). While the expression "types and symbols" often relates the two concepts closely, there is a basic distinction. The former always refers to an antitype future to itself; the latter may have a past, present, or future reference. The essential mark of symbolism is human participation in the reality suggested by the symbol.[28] It has the power to clarify, to compress into a single, meaningful entity that is easily grasped and retained; thus it provides a center to shape conduct and faith.[29]

When interpreting symbols, the following principles have value: (a) Understand the names of symbols literally; for example, a tree, a horn, or a chariot are literal or natural designations of what the writer saw or thought. (b) Symbols point to something different from themselves, directing one to a lesson or truth. (c) Discover what the writer was trying to convey by using the symbol.

As might be expected, many biblical symbols occur in the

prophetic and the apocalyptic books (Daniel and Revelation). Sometimes they are identified within the book; otherwise we must search for clues in other biblical or extra-biblical writings. See the visions of Amos 7–9, Zechariah 1–6, Daniel 7–12 or the Apocalypse (Revelation).

There are symbols like the cherubim (Gen. 3:24), the burning bush (Exod. 3:2–3), the pillar of cloud and fire (Exod. 13:31–32), or "the living creatures" (Ezek. 1:5–14; Rev. 4:6–8). There are symbols like blood, sometimes identified as a "life-principle" (Lev. 17:14), as the basis for atonement (Lev. 17:11), or as the remission of sins (Heb. 9:22).

Such things as numbers (three, four, ten, twelve), colors (white, red, black, yellow-green), metals (gold, silver, bronze, iron), and precious stones (topaz, rubies), abound in the Bible. Notice the "sevens" running through the Apocalypse (1:4, 12, 16; 5:6; 6:1, etc.), the various horses in Zechariah (1:8; 6:2), the metals composing the image in Daniel (2:32–33), or the gems in the breastplate of the high priest (Exod. 28:17–20).

On occasion the symbol takes the form of a pun or word-play (in the Hebrew or Greek texts). Jeremiah sees "a rod of almond" *shaked*, which is a symbol of the Lord's vigilance: "for I am watching [*shoked*] over my word to perform it" (Jer. 1:11, 12). Again, "a basket of summer fruit" *qayits* symbolizes "the end" *qets* as the judgment of the Lord comes upon Israel (Amos 8:1, 2).

It is important to recognize the principle of the context in identifying the meaning of symbols. McQuilkin has noted the symbol of leaven in two contexts in the gospel of Matthew, in each case representing a different meaning.[30] In 16:6 Jesus warned his disciples against "the leaven of the Pharisees and Sadducees," referring to their teaching (v. 12), which he had criticized earlier (15:1–11). But in 13:33 leaven is a symbol of the pervasive influence of the good news which brings about the spread of the kingdom of God. (This is a caution to the interpreter not to "freeze" a symbol, insisting that it has the same meaning in every occurrence.)

Finally, objects used as symbols (stones, numbers, fire, water, etc.) in the Bible do not always carry symbolic meaning. Once again we shall have to apply the guidelines for dealing with literal and figurative language. For example, the word "well" in John 4:6 appears to be literal, whereas in 4:14 it is a symbol of the life-giving provision that Jesus offered. Again, the names Sidon and Egypt are commonly used in the Bible for physical locations, whereas in Rev. 11:8 the names are used "spiritually" for the place "where our Lord was crucified."

Common figures of speech

Once more the basic guidelines for ascertaining the meaning of figurative language will be useful: would a literal meaning fit into the writer's description or message? Is there a reason for a figurative sense? Do history and grammar support it?

The most common categories are metaphor and simile. In fact, Caird says that "for our immediate purpose it is useful to regard them as interchangeable," and he cites the standard *Modern English Usage* by H. W. Fowler as support ("every metaphor presupposes a simile, and every simile is compressible or convertible into a metaphor").[31] Under these two categories he arranges most of the other forms of comparison.

The following eight examples of common figures of speech will indicate their importance to interpretation.

(1) Metaphor (literally, "to transfer")—application of a name, descriptive term, or phrase to an object or action to which it is not literally applicable (for example, "food for thought"): "all flesh is grass" (Isa. 40:6); "his faithfulness is a shield and buckler" (Ps. 91:4); "For sin, finding opportunity in the commandment, deceived me and by it killed me" (Rom. 7:11). While the metaphor is not as close to the fact as the simile, it is closer to feeling. There is an intensity involved in these statements, and the comparisons often tend to be striking. (See also Matt. 5:13; Gal. 2:9; Heb. 12:1.)

In Rom. 7:11, "sin" is practically personified, and it seized an opportunity to deceive and kill. The passage is parallel to Gen. 3:1ff., where the serpent seized an opportunity to deceive Eve, bringing death upon her (and Adam) (see Gen. 2:17; 3:3–4). In "opportunity" *aphorme* we have literally, "the starting point or base of operations for a military expedition" (*Arndt and Gingrich*). It came to mean an "occasion, pretext, or opportunity." In "killed" the word usually applied to physical death is used of a spiritual condition.

A modern illustration of metaphor appears in the poem entitled "On a Clergyman's Horse Biting Him":

> The steed bit his master;
> How came this to pass?
> He heard the good pastor
> Cry, "All flesh is grass."[32]

(2) Simile (literally, "like")—reference to a thing or person, with explicit comparison to it of what is being discussed (for example, "as dead as a doornail"): "All flesh is like grass" (1 Pet. 1:24); "thou dost cover him with favor as with a shield" (Ps. 5:12); or a multiple simile,

> And the daughter of Zion is left
> like a booth in a vineyard,
> like a lodge in a cucumber field,
> like a besieged city (Isa. 1:8).

The simile thus expresses the comparison, whereas the metaphor makes a direct transfer, simply implying the comparison. (Notice that, in the first two examples above, the same elements are used as in the metaphor examples.) Some similes reflect strong emotions, such as loneliness or deep affection:

> I am like a desert owl,
> like an owl among the ruins.
> I lie awake,
> I have become like a bird alone
>   on a housetop (Ps. 102:6–7 NIV).

(3) Hyperbole (literally, "excess")—an exaggerated statement not meant to be taken literally: "You see that you can do nothing; look, the whole world has gone after him" (John 12:19); (Some take this to be synecdoche instead; that is, "world" meaning "multitudes of people of all sorts," using the whole for its parts.) "and their camels were without number, as the sand which is upon the seashore for multitude" (Judg. 7:12); "Every night I flood my bed with tears; I drench my couch with my weeping" (Ps. 6:6); "His heart is hard as a stone, hard as the nether millstone" (Job 41:24).

Hyperbole is not like "a fish story." One does not expect to be believed, but is adding emphasis to the real message. In his famous poem "A Red, Red Rose," R. Burns promises to love his "bonnie lass" till all the seas go dry, and the rocks melt with the sun! Even though he must leave her for awhile, he will come to her again, even though it were "ten thousand mile."

In the ancient nation of Israel, the tribe of Benjamin was the smallest in number, yet for warfare their fierceness and ability was second to none. They had seven hundred choice warriors, "every one could sling a stone at a hair, and not miss" (Judg. 20:16). Again, deep affection could be expressed by the churches of Galatia for the apostle Paul. "For I bear you witness," he wrote to them, "that, if possible, you would have plucked out your eyes and given them to me" (Gal. 4:15).

(4) Synecdoche (literally, "to receive from")—a part is named but the whole is understood (100 "head" for 100 "cattle"), or the whole is named but a part is understood (Minnesota beat Chicago at football): "And afterwards I shall see his face" (Gen. 32:20); "the Lord loves the gates of Zion" (Ps. 87:2); "in the temple, where all Jews come together" (John 18:20, meaning a particular part of the temple complex); "that all the world should be enrolled" (Luke 2:1, world meaning the Roman Empire). In poetic expressions some telling or colorful examples of synecdoche occur. According to a literal rendering of the Hebrew text in Deut. 32:41, "If I sharpen the lightning of my sword, and my hand takes hold of

judgment," the flashing gleam of the sword stands for its sharp edge, and the Lord's hand represents his authoritative victory. In the expression, "In the day when the keepers of the house tremble" (Eccl. 12:3), the singular "day" stands for a particular period of time. There is much similarity between synecdoche and metonymy, so that distinction is often difficult. Some prefer to merge the two under the heading of metonymy.

(5) Metonymy (literally, "to change a name")—a substitution of the name of an attribute or adjunct for that of the thing itself ("crown" for 'king"): "And beginning with Moses and all the prophets" (Luke 24:27, meaning the writings of the Old Testament); "Then went out to him Jerusalem and all Judea and all the region about the Jordan" (Matt. 3:5, meaning the people of those localities); "Who say to a tree, 'You are my father'" (Jer. 2:27, referring to an idol made from a tree). The prophecy concerning the king's steward Eliakim (Isa. 22:22) included the clause, "And I will place on his shoulder the key of the house of David," where the word "key" represented his authority over the king's household, and "upon his shoulder" was a symbol of the heavy responsibility which he would carry. The "scepter" (Gen. 49:10) was a way of stating royal dominion.

In Shakespeare's poem "Spring," he wrote of the cuckoo bird's song as "Unpleasing to a married ear," meaning married men. A. Noyes' poem "the Highway-man" includes the line, "As the black cascade of perfume came tumbling over his breast," a reference to his sweetheart's long black hair.

(6) Irony (literally, "a dissembling"; "simulated ignorance") —using language of an opposite or different tendency, as simulated adoption of another's point of view or laudatory tone for purpose of ridicule: "You have a fine way of rejecting the commandment of God, in order to keep your tradition!" (Mark 7:9); "the lordly price at which I was paid off by them" (Zech. 11:13); "No doubt you are the people, and wisdom will die with you" (Job 12:2).

Irony may come close to, or even include, such elements as sarcasm, ridicule or satire, but these are not essential to it.

Best when subtle, it adds larger dimensions to meaning. Perrine distinguishes three kinds of irony: (a) verbal irony, (b) dramatic irony, and (c) irony of situation.[33] An example of (a) is found in Job 12:2 (see above); an example of (b) appears in Esth. 6:6, where the king's question to Haman does not apply to him at all but to his rival Mordecai; and an example of (c) may be seen in Luke 24:32, as the disciples realize that the "stranger" on the road was in reality the Lord Jesus.

(7) Litotes (literally, "plain" or "meager")—an ironical understatement, expressing an affirmative by the negative of its contrary ("no small" problem, for "a great" problem): "and we seemed to ourselves like grasshoppers, and so we seemed to them" (Num. 13:33); "But I am a worm, and no man" (Ps. 22:6); "But now for a brief moment favor has been shown by the Lord our God...that our God may brighten our eyes and grant us a little reviving in our bondage" (Ezra 9:8; here he magnifies the grace of God in contrast to the long time of oppression); "I am the least of the apostles, unfit to be called an apostle" (1 Cor. 15:9; compare 2 Cor. 11:5; 12:11–12). Caird notes that Luke in the book of Acts is "particularly fond of the use of the negative with expressions of quantity or quality":[34] see "no small stir" (12:18); "no little business" (19:24); "not disobedient to" (26:19); and "no small tempest" (27:20), among others. This is essentially opposite of hyperbole.

(8) Euphemism (literally, "good speaking")—a substitution of a mild, vague, or roundabout expression for a harsh, blunt, or direct one ("domestic engineer" for "housewife"): "you shall go to your fathers in peace" (Gen. 15:15, meaning you shall die); "If the Lord had not been my help, my soul would soon have dwelt in the land of silence" (Ps. 94:17); "for he himself knew what was in man" (John 2:25); "those who have fallen asleep" (1 Thess. 4:14, meaning they have died).

Frequently euphemism was used to avoid being indelicate about personal or sexual matters. Elijah's mocking words about Baal, "he has gone aside" (1 Kin. 18:27), or a description of one "relieving himself" (Judg. 3:24), were common euphemisms. So also such expressions as "to uncover nakedness" (Lev. 18:6ff.) related to cohabitation, and even referred to contracting marriage. For a man to "know" his wife was to have sexual relations with her (Gen. 4:1; Matt. 1:25).

CHAPTER NINE

Historical and Cultural Context

THE STUDENT OF the Bible needs a knowledge of history, geography, chronology, and antiquities; particularly "a clear conception of the order of events connected with the whole course of sacred history." One needs also to gain acquaintance with "the customs, life, spirit, ideas and pursuits" of those different periods of history and the nations involved. Such insights will enable one to understand the biblical period, and aid in not confusing the idea of one age or race with another.[1]

As we read the Bible, we are continually confronted by events, dates, times and numbers, and names of people and places, along with many references to customs and cultures. From this data it is fairly evident that the Bible was written within a historical/cultural framework. Yet we need also to see how the biblical narrative transcends its cultural milieu. A little book by G. E. Wright entitled *The Old Testament Against Its Environment* (1950) gives a rather vivid picture of the uniqueness of the religion of Israel among the religious culture of the ancient Near East.

But aside from a study of history and culture in itself, we need to see the similarities and the differences between these elements in the biblical text and in the present day, so as to carry over the biblical message to each new generation. How do we get from God's message in the Bible to God's message today? How can the words of Scripture come alive in the words of a contemporary preacher or teacher? E. Best has stated it with conviction: "We want to interpret Scripture so that we come to an understanding of God and ourselves. We want to unleash the Word that is in Scripture so that it becomes God's word to us today."[2] In the following sections we present illustrations of how knowledge about history and culture contribute to the interpretation process.

Historical context

The Old Testament is the story of Israel; the New Testament the story of Jesus Christ and his earliest followers. But this is a history with an added dimension, for "in the Bible it is God's Spirit which intervenes in human affairs, which manifests his power and which (through the prophets) makes plain his will, his demands, and his unmerited grace."[3]

What are some of the features that can help us to grasp the sweep of this story, thus giving a better understanding of what occurred, and a more acute sense of the relation of the parts to the whole?

(1) Aspects of the nature of biblical history. A basic starting point is the area of biblical history and its encompassing geography. To put it popularly, "When and where did things happen?" The purpose of this aspect of study is to gain a context for the text itself.

What is "history"? No longer can we speak about "bare facts," for there is no such thing for the historian. Two standard definitions are: (a) "events in time and space that have social significance";[4] and (b) "an event together with the (inevitable) interpretation that enters into the recollecting and recording of it."[5]

In the twentieth century, a more positive estimate of the materials has arisen. This follows the controversies of the previous two centuries, when biblical "history" tended to be discredited or suspect in many quarters. The rehabilitation of the credibility of the biblical narratives is one of the most outstanding gains, coming both from archaeological and textual studies.[6]

C. R. North has analyzed methods of historical writing in the Bible as follows:[7]

(a) Narrative, usually in the form of annals; that is, materials drawn from various records or collections. We see frequently in the Old Testament reference to "the Book of the Chronicles of the Kings of Israel" (1 Kin. 14:19) or, "the Book of the Chronicles of the Kings of Judah" (1 Kin. 14:29). While some Old Testament materials are often highly moralistic (pointing out especially the evils of the people), the narratives in 2 Samuel 9 to 1 Kings. 2 (of the reign of David) tend to be quite objective and do not moralize.

(b) Didactic, which is "history with a purpose." This can be seen in Deuteronomy, Judges, and Kings, which are "more concerned to point out the moral for their contemporaries than to give an unbiased account of the past."

(c) Scientific, usually referring to "pure history" in the modern sense, which does not moralize, yet may contain a distinct "philosophy of history." What we see in the Old Testament is historical material written from "the perspective of eternity"—as would appear in the pentateuchal stories and in the prophetic writings.

Old Testament narratives do not pretend to be complete; they are often highly selective. For example, in the books of Chronicles, much material is omitted that occurs in Samuel and Kings—the records of the reigns of the kings of Israel (the Northern kingdom) are completely omitted. Often unpleasant details concerning the kings are passed over (compare 1 Chron. 20:1 with 2 Sam. 11:1–12:26). The Chronicler appears to have omitted materials that did not suit his purpose. Yet a recent verdict is that "within the limits of its purpose, the Chronicler's story is accurate whenever it can be checked, though the method of presentation is homiletical."[8] The only major problem remaining is the use of numbers in these books, which often (not always) are much larger than the parallels in Samuel and Kings.

(2) History of the ancient Near East. Israel's history was not spent in isolation from surrounding peoples. Some of the nations round about were older and more complex civilizations, and there were many points of contact between them.[9]

One of these great civilizations was Mesopotamia, which

lay to the east of the land of Palestine. Entering the southern sector of the Tigris-Euphrates River valley about 3300 B.C., the Sumerians invented and developed the art of cuneiform (wedge-shaped) writing. They also developed a cosmology (study of the universe) and a theology which became basic dogma for the whole of the Near East. According to this view the four gods created everything by "the divine word" and fashioned man from clay, a creature who was to serve the gods with food, drink and shelter.

In the third millennium B.C., the land of Sumer consisted of about twelve city-states, each of which was marked by a *ziggurat,* or religious stage-tower, called "Sumer's most characteristic contribution to religious architecture." (Compare the so-called Tower of Babel in Gen. 11:1–9, which some believe refers to the famous Temple of Marduk, the chief god of ancient Babylon. It was from this location, the land of Shinar [Sumer?] that humans were scattered and the confusion of languages took place.)

By the middle of the twenty-first century B.C., a legal code had been compiled by Ur-Nammu, a Sumerian king. A city governor administered the laws for the city. Between about 2000–1720 B.C. there was a strong Semitic influence in the territory of Ur. By 1770, Hammurabi had become the sole ruler of the states of Sumer and Akkad, giving prominence to the Semitic culture. (In the Bible, the Semites were descendants of Noah's son Shem; see Gen. 10:21–31; 11:10–26, eventuating in the family of Abraham, 11:27–32.)

Another of the great cultures was that of Egypt, to the south of Palestine. Between 3100–2100 B.C. urban centers developed rapidly and great building projects were undertaken (the pyramids at Gizeh). During the period 2100–1500 B.C. there were contacts with the land of Canaan (Palestine); the accounts describe the land as "a good land, abundant in figs, grapes, wine, honey and olives (compare Exod. 3:8; Deut. 8:8). From 1500–1200 B.C., following the expulsion of the foreign Hyksos peoples who had invaded Egypt about 1700, the kingdom of Egypt attained its greatest splendor. Thutmose

III (1490–1436), who some see as "the Pharaoh of the Exodus," was the greatest conqueror of all the Egyptian kings, and controlled the land from Egypt to the Euphrates River. Amenhotep IV (Akhenaten) between 1364–1347 was a noted religious reformer. The thirteenth century King Rameses II was a famous builder (see Exod. 1:11). By this period we are well within the time of the liberation of the Hebrew people from slavery in Egypt, and we can follow their departure up to the land of Canaan. Though it is impossible to be detailed here some study of the history of this early period by the student will give background and setting for the rise and development of the Hebrew nation.

(3) Stages in Israel's history. Closely tied to the history of the patriarchs (see Genesis 12–50) is the theme of the land. This is both a physical reality and symbolic of a decision to enter history, to set out upon a pilgrimage.[10]

Abraham was given the promise of a name and a nation (Gen. 12:1–3). Then came a hint of the identity of the land (see Gen. 15:7, "this land," and vv. 17–21). We see, too, an emphasis on God's intent—his promise (Gen.17:2, 6; notice the word "exceedingly")—accompanied by the "focal verse of the tradition of promise history" (v. 8).

The history goes on with Isaac and Jacob (see particularly Gen. 35:1–4) and concludes with Joseph, one of the sons (who will become "the twelve tribes of Israel"). Even in his death, Joseph is destined for "a place of promise" (Gen. 50:25).

Following the settlement of the Hebrews in Egypt under Joseph (where they had the best of the land, security, and prosperity; Gen. 47:6, 17), we read of the Exodus under Moses, the giving of the Law, the conquest of Canaan under Joshua, the days of the judges (legal-military figures in Canaan), and the rise of the monarchy (1 Samuel–2 Kings). Rule by kings, first over a united kingdom (Saul, David, and Solomon), was followed by two sets of kings (in the north, Israel, and in the south, Judah). These kingdoms ended in disasters, the north falling to Assyria in 722 B.C., the south to

Babylon in 586 B.C. Only a small band of settlers returned to Judah, rebuilding the Temple in 515 B.C. (the edifice built by Solomon had been destroyed by the Babylonians), and later finding a degree of community under Ezra and Nehemiah about the middle of the fifth century B.C. Thus the Old Testament period came to its conclusion.[11]

History and geography will blend in a study of the life of Abraham. The data should be carefully studied concerning his travels from Ur to Haran (Gen. 11:31), to the land of Canaan (12:5), to places within the land, such as Shechem (12:6), Bethel and Ai (12:8), and the Negeb (v. 9). Then we see him in Egypt (12:10–20), back to the Negeb (13:1), to Bethel (13:3), and to Hebron (13:18). We are told of a rapid journey "as far as Dan" (14:14) and to Hobah, north of Damascus (14:15), followed by his return to "the King's Valley" (14:17), and to Hebron again. Some time later he journeyed, dwelling between Kadesh and Shur, sojourning in Gerar (20:1) "many days" (21:34). Following is his travel to "the land of Moriah" (22:2), and a return to Beer-sheba (22:19). Both he and Sarah died and were buried in the cave of Macpelah at Hebron (23:19; 25:9).

The reader may ask why this data is significant. Possibly a preliminary question ought to be about the meaning of these names, not simply lexically but in terms of the kind of place and conditions they represent. And what did the writer mean to convey by listing a series of journeyings and sojournings, together with accompanying events? Surely the framework, if framework it is, for the "life of Abraham" has definite meaning.[12] Several factors may be mentioned here.

(a) Attention should be given to the historical background of Genesis 12–25 (or even through chap. 50). There had been disruptions in Mesopotamia, from which Abraham had come, due to Amorite invasions during the early part of the second millennium B.C. Babylon, Mari, and Haran were subjugated. Also, Gen. 12:6 notes, "at that time the Canaanites were in the land," and one of their sacred centers was at Shechem, where Abraham first built an altar to the Lord (12:7).

(b) Again, the pattern of Abraham's journeys in these chapters recurs later in connection with Jacob's travels. See especially 12:6 with 33:18; 12:7 with 33:20; 12:8 with 28:11, 13, 18; 13:4 with 35:7; 13:15 with 35:12; and 13:18 with 35:8, 27. B. Vawter has noted that "a certain standardization had been imposed on the narrative," and it featured locales religiously significant to the Israelites— Shechem, Bethel, and Mamre.[13]

(c) There is evident within these narratives a blending of the human and divine activities. Abraham travels "as the Lord told him" (12:4). He "called on the name of the Lord," built altars to him, and responded to his words and commands (15:6; 22:1ff.). In turn God appeared to him, spoke, and made covenant with him.

As another type of narrative we may turn to a segment of the life of David, a story which will illustrate and interpret God's care over his life. In 1 Samuel 19–26 are recorded seven threats against David's life by King Saul: 19:1, 10, 11; 19:20a; 20:1, 31; 23:7; 23:15, 26; 24:2; 26:2, 20. In each case some person or circumstance was instrumental in rescuing David from Saul's intent to kill him: Saul's daughter Michal (David's wife) rescued him; "the Spirit of God" came upon Saul; David was delivered by Saul's son Jonathan; Abiathar the priest rescued him; a raid by the Philistines upset Saul's plans; finally, God's judgment against Saul turned him away from his evil intent.

Brief historical narratives such as these offer the reader an opportunity to deal with history as narrated from a dual perspective. There the events of human life are told and interpreted from the standpoint of divine promise and intervention.

(4) Historical setting of the New Testament. One helpful approach to the study of the New Testament is to establish the historical setting for its writings. An important contribution to this has been made by the books of Luke and Acts, covering the period from the birth of Christ to the Roman imprisonment of Paul (ca. 6/5 B.C.–A.D. 62). This can be seen in a chronological-geographical sequence as follows:

a. the birth and early years of Jesus (Luke 1:1–4:15).
b. Jesus in Galilee (Luke 4:16–9:50).
c. Jesus in Perea (Luke 9:51–18:30).
d. Jesus in Jerusalem (Luke 18:31–24:53).
e. the apostles in Jerusalem (Acts 1:1–8:3).
f. the apostles in Samaria and Judea (Acts 8:4–11:18).
g. the apostles in the Mediterranean world (Acts 11:9–21:14).
h. the imprisonments of Paul in Jerusalem, Caesarea, and Rome (Acts 21:15–28:31).

During this period Palestine (and the Roman world) was under the rule of Roman or Roman-appointed officials. Notice how Luke highlights some of these in his gospel (1:5; 2:1–2; 3:1–2; 23:1–17) and in Acts (11:28; 12:1, 20–23; 13:7; 18:12–17; 23:26; 24:27; 25:10–12, 13, 23–27). These and other examples will aid one in seeing the extent to which early Christianity was a part of the Roman world. The drama involving the life of Christ and the early disciples "was not done in a corner" (compare Acts 26:26).

It is striking to realize that Christ's birth was recorded in relation to a Roman-appointed king, Herod the Great (37–34 B.C.), ruler of Palestine, and a Roman emperor, Caesar Augustus (27 B.C.–A.D. 14); that his public ministry was carried out in the framework of the reign of Tiberius Caesar (A.D. 14–37), and Herod Antipas (4 B.C.–A.D. 39), tetrarch of Galilee; and that he was tried and executed by Pontius Pilate (A.D. 26–36), Roman prefect of Judea, and Joseph Caiaphas (A.D. 18–36), high priest of the Jewish nation. Was this all purely "historical" and "political"? Not according to the words of Acts 4:27–28:

> For truly in this city there were gathered together against thy holy servant Jesus, whom thou didst anoint, both Herod and Pontius Pilate, with the Gentiles and the peoples of Israel, to do whatever thy hand and thy plan had predestined to take place.

In the preface to his *New Testament History,* Professor F. F. Bruce adds: "New Testament history is indeed charged with theological implications ... (and) the theological implications can be the better appreciated when the historical basis is duly laid."[14]

Another approach to historical setting is to study the letters of Paul along with their background as described in the book of Acts. Suppose one reads Paul's letter to Thessalonica (1 Thessalonians). What is its historical context? We turn first to the letter itself for any clues. There are indications of Paul's visit among them, and of his reception and relations to them (1:9; 2:10, 11); also the circumstances surrounding his visit (2:14–16; 3:1–10). Then the background of the history is filled out by Acts 17:1–9, a narrative of Paul's visit to the city. He sees the conflict in the synagogue, caused by Paul's preaching that Jesus was the Messiah (17:3), and the charges against Paul and Silas that they were troublemakers; they had opposed the decrees of Caesar by heralding "another king, Jesus" (17:6–7). In addition, any good Bible encyclopedia article on "Thessalonica" will fill in details of the history, culture and political situation of the day. Books on New Testament archaeology will likewise be helpful. All together this data will make the reading of the epistle much more "meaning-full."[15] It must be remembered, too, that this single epistle is part of the Pauline corpus of letters; also, that the whole of Paul's "missionary journeys" should be studied to see the place of Thessalonica within the larger picture.

This sort of procedure can be used also with Paul's letters to the Galatians (Acts 13:14–14:28) and to the Philippians (Acts 19:1–41; 20:17–38). A careful study of these passages and the contents of each letter, supplemented by books on New Testament history and Bible dictionary articles, will give a sense of the inter-relatedness of the literature, the historical and cultural framework, and the theological messages contained therein.

Cultural context

There is not a rigid division between the cultural context and the historical which we have just examined.[16] Certainly the history of Abraham was within the culture of his day, even as that of Paul and the Thessalonians was within theirs. Yet it may be convenient to deal with each separately for purposes of analysis. B. Ramm defines "cultural" as "the total ways, methods, manners, tools, customs, buildings, institutions, and so forth, by means of which, and through which, a clan, tribe, or a nation carry on their existence."[17]

We can readily experience "culture-shock" today as we travel to other countries—where customs, language, food, transportation, and many other things, may be quite different from our own. Such a simple matter of properly greeting another person may suddenly become a matter of great perplexity—do you speak, shake hands, embrace, rub noses, or bow?

Similarly, we may well experience culture-shock in reading the Bible. "Reclining at table," "lighting a lamp," customs of marriage, hair styles, participation in a synogogue service, eating meat offered to idols, regulations for planting seeds—all of these and hundreds of other matters will either not be understood or will be misunderstood.

One of the best sources of information on the many and varied aspects of biblical cultures is the *Harper's Encyclopedia of Bible Life* (third revised edition, 1978). It deals with the world of the Bible, how the people of the Bible lived, and how they earned their livelihoods. Here one is familiarized with homes, food, clothing, jewelry, medicine, family events, and religious events. Then one learns of the life of the nomad, the farmer, and the professional person, along with the aspects of civil, military, and industrial life.

To illustrate some cultural aspects of the Bible, we shall take samples from several different areas.

(1) Housing. From early times in Israel tents were commonly used as housing. Normally a tent was composed of nine poles, set in three parallel rows of three each, the middle row being about seven feet high, higher than the outside rows. Across these was stretched a black goat-hair cover, the sides being rolled up in warm weather. Often a tent was divided into two "apartments," the back part occupied by the women and children. We read in the Bible of such famous tent

dwellers as Abraham (Gen. 12:8; 18:1–15) and tent makers as the apostle Paul (Acts 18:1–3). Sometimes wealthy families had separate tents for the wife and the servants. The most famous tent in the Bible was the Tabernacle, "the Tent in the Wilderness" (Exod. 40:18–33).

Later on permanent housing became more common. The average Israelite house was constructed usually of mud-brick, having a thatched roof supported by heavy beams below. The thatch was covered with mud and clay, and rolled until it was flat and hard. This was the most popular part of the dwelling, and was used for drying grain, eating, praying or sleeping. One can better understand, then, how "thieves could break through (literally, dig through) a wall and steal (Matt. 6:20); or how people could "remove" a roof (Mark 2:4). Roofs were used as holy places (Jer. 19:13) or for prayer-times (Acts 10:9). More elaborate stuctures might have guest rooms on the roof (2 Kin. 4:10) or "upper rooms" (Luke 22:12).

(2) Marriage customs. In a patriarchal society, descent was reckoned from the father, and the father gave the name to the newborn child, thus transmitting the essence of his life to the descendant (Gen. 5:3, 29; Exod. 2:22). Monogamy is often assumed in the Old Testament (Gen. 2:24; Eccl. 9:9), although there were polygamous marriages, often for economic or political reasons (Gen. 29:18, 25, 30; 2 Sam. 5:13). In the New Testament, monogamy is the normal arrangement, and overseers in the church had to be "the husband of one wife" (1 Tim. 3:2).

Marriage was based on a covenant (Prov. 2:17; Mal. 2:14), initiated by the father of the son (Josh. 15:16; Gen. 24:4). Normally this was arranged by a "marriage present," called a *mohar* (Gen. 34:12). It is not clear whether this involved the actual "sale" of a woman, so that she became the husband's "property" (compare Exod. 20:17), or whether the term better referred to compensation paid to the family for wrong done to them (Gen. 34:7). (There were other cases where a daughter was sold; see Exod. 21:7–11).

The betrothal was a private arrangement between the

parents and binding upon the parties involved (1 Sam. 18:21). As we see in Matt. 1:18–19, the relationship was to be broken by divorce, so that it seems to have had the binding force of marriage. The marriage state was regarded highly by Paul, as he used it as a figure of Christ and the Church (Eph. 5:23–33).

(3) Climate and its effects. Israel was an agricultural society, claiming land as its most precious possession and depending on the soil for food. The cycle of agriculture was determined by seasonal changes.

A famous inscription in the Hebrew language, dating from the eleventh to the tenth centuries B.C., was discovered in southern Palestine in 1908. It is called the Gezer Calendar and details the agricultural cycle:

> His two months are [olive] harvest (Sept.–Nov.)
> His two months are planting [grain] (Nov.–Jan.)
> His two months are late planting (Jan.–Mar.)
> His month is hoeing up of flax (Mar.–Apr.)
> His month is harvest of barley (Apr.–May)
> His month is harvest and feasting (May–June)
> His two months are vine-tending (June–Aug.)
> His month is summer fruit (Aug.–Sept.)

Translated by W. F. Albright, this (school) lesson lays out the yearly schedule for farming. The dry season lasted from May to October, the wet season from November to April. The "early rains" came before mid-November (Joel 2:23); the stormy season from December to March (Song 2:11); and the latter rains in April and May (Jer. 3:3). If the rains failed to arrive, it meant hardship for all (Jer. 14:1–6).

Seed was generally sown by hand. A careful farmer would waste little seed by sowing it upon prepared land (Isa. 28:23–26); others sowed it before plowing, thus it could be lost to birds or to natural forces (see Mark 4:3–7). Barley was harvested in April; wheat in May. The most important crop, the grape, was harvested in early autumn, usually September. Coinciding with these harvests were the three great religious festivals—Passover, Pentecost and Tabernacles (Booths). The religious aspects of these celebrations are detailed in Leviticus 23.

These physical factors also affected other aspects of the life of biblical people. The dry season was the usual time for warfare (1 Chron. 20:1); the wet season (heavy rains) could be precarious (Judg. 5:21), as in the case of a river overflowing its banks. Sea travel also was dangerous during the winter, due to tempestuous winds sweeping from the northeast across the Mediterranean Sea (Acts 27:14–15). (Notice that Acts 27:9–12 indicates the soon arrival of "winter.")

Within Palestine water was a precious commodity. Cisterns were dug to hold huge supplies of water; cities and villages would be located near a spring. It was looked upon as "a good land, a land of brooks of water, of fountains and springs, flowing forth in valleys and hills" (Deut. 8:7). Thus, the Lord was called "Israel's fountain" (Ps. 68:26). Jesus offered "living water" to those who believed in him (John 4:14; 7:38). Even today some of these ancient springs are the water source for residents of that land, as is the Gibon spring and Pool of Siloam in Jerusalem, and the Virgin's Fountain in Nazareth.

(4) The importance of a knowledge of biblical culture. It is not that we study culture as an end in itself, interesting though it may be to some. Rather, we want to gain an appreciation of what God is saying to us in the Bible, yet not be puzzled or distracted by certain items that are strange to us from our cultural perspective. Some of the difficulties that arise in understanding the Bible are due to our lack of understanding many of the customs and aspects of those days.

The potential list is virtually endless, due both to words that mean little to us now or customs that are strange to our life-styles. To some reader, words (or customs and languages) like "alms," "coals of fire," "devouring widows' houses," "proclaiming upon the housetops," "shutteth up his bowels," "Simon the Canaanean," or "Simon Zelotes," are quite strange.

They may mean nothing at all or they may call up false images. Why did Paul write, "It is well for a man not to touch a woman" (1 Cor. 7:1)? Why should one not eat food "offered to idols"? How long is "long hair"? What is "a yoke of slavery"? Why was Barnabas called a "good" man? What is an "apt teacher"? What did "the laying on of hands" signify? Is "a little wine" always good for stomach ailments?

To get at such problems the handiest tool is a good Bible Dictionary, or a book on Bible customs. Try *The New Bible Dictionary*, (2nd Edition), *The Zondervan Pictorial Encyclopedia of the Bible*, and *Harper's Encyclopedia of Bible Life.*

Sometimes we find clues within the biblical texts themselves or in literature of the biblical period. This can be a help in getting at some issues. Did people in Israel offer food to the dead? One text seems to indicate that: "I have not...offered any of it (the tithe) to the dead" (Deut. 24:14); does this imply others did? We know it was a practice in Egypt, and it may have been a Canaanite custom, too (offered to Ba'al, the "Dead One"). Later on it became a custom in Israel, at least among the exiles (see Tobit 4:17). But at an earlier stage it was apparently prohibited in Israel (Deut. 14:1), and our text is probably to be taken as a strong affirmation that the person has not defiled the tithe by participation in a pagan rite.[18]

In the Bible salt was used to season food (Job 6:6; Ezra 6:9); a "covenant of salt" was a sign of fellowship and friendship (Num. 18:19; Ezra 4:14); all cereal offerings to the Lord required salt (Lev. 2:13). How could salt "lose its savor"? (Matt. 5:13): possibly by being mixed with foreign matter (other chemicals), thus no longer retaining the power of pure salt.[19]

We see in the Gospels the use of the two titles "King of the Jews" and "King of Israel." Often they are used interchangeably, as having only a difference in form, not in significance. Yet a review of the instances will show that the title "King of the Jews" is used by non-Jews only while the title "King of Israel" is used by Jews only. The wise men from the East (Matt. 2:2) and Pilate and the Roman soldiers (Matt. 27:11,

27, 29, 37, and parallels in Mark 15, Luke 23, and John 18–19) used the former; Nathaniel (John 1:49), the crowd in Jerusalem (John 12:13), and the Jewish leaders (Matt. 27:42, parallel to Mark 15:32) used the latter. Why the distinction? The "King of the Jews" was regarded as a political title; the "King of Israel" as a messianic title. Thus the latter would be quite appropriate for Jewish usage, but not for the politically-minded Romans.[20] Further, Herod the Great had been awarded the title "the King of the Jews" by Caesar Augustus,[21] thus it may not have been appropriate for Jews to use it of anyone else, especially of Jesus of Nazareth.

As a final illustration we look at a term describing the Jewish law as "schoolmaster" (KJV), or "custodian" (RSV), or "tutor" (NASB) (Gal. 3:24). The term in the Greek text is *paidagogos*—literally, "one who leads a child." Rather than an educational function, the word points to strict supervision and moral direction of a child. The pedagogue in this culture was a slave, often an older man, who was employed to exercise a general moral supervision over a young boy, and was responsible for both his physical and moral well-being. Thus the pedagogue was "a fit emblem of the Mosaic law," and the word was used in an interesting rabbinic paraphrase of Num. 11:12 for "a nursing father."[22] Paul used the same term again in 1 Cor. 4:15 to contrast himself as "a spiritual father" with the many "guides" (RSV) or "tutors" (NASB) of the Corinthian believers.[23]

From these and other examples, a number of broad principles for attempting to hear the Word of God in its historically and enculturated form may be suggested.[24]

(a) Cultivate an awareness of the general similarities and distinctions between the biblical world and the modern world.

(b) Be alert to the diversity of the historical/cultural within the scope of the biblical writings. There are contrasts between Hebrew culture and Greek culture; there are many social and political backgrounds (Hebrew, Egyptian, Mesopotamian, Greek, Roman, etc.).

(c) Look for evidences within the writings which define

specific cultural expressions, or which identify historical events, persons, institutions, or customs.

(d) Relate Old Testament backgrounds to New Testament texts. Do the same within each Testament (for example, the relation of the historical books to the prophets; or, the relation of the book of Acts to the epistles).

(e) Is there "more to the text" than the cultural situation will show? Does the author say something that transcends his own cultural situation? What is there in the text that speaks to people beyond the immediate circumstances and context?

Such a discipline will be useful in facing up to our own prejudices and preconceived interpretations. We can get new insights into both historical and contemporary aspects and values of the Bible.

CHAPTER TEN

Theological Context

THE BIBLE IS a theological book; that is, it brings to the reader a message about God. That message is given through the history, poetry, prophecies, gospels, letters, and apocalypses found within its pages. Thus we call the Bible "the Word of God."

The principle of revelation

If we look for some "organizing center" in our interpretation of the Bible (and many have been suggested, such as covenant, promise, religion, etc.), we simply cannot afford to overlook the concept of revelation:

> Neither the New Testament nor the Old makes sense any longer if we abandon the concept of revelation and . . . interpret what prophets and apostles experienced as the insights of religious genius rather than the disclosure of a radically different dimension to human existence.[1]

When referring to the Bible as "the Word of God" we mean he has revealed himself to us; it is a divinely-given literature. Further, we have noted that this revelation was given within the historical context of the life of Israel, culminating in the life and teachings of Jesus Christ—"God spoke of old to our fathers by the prophets; but in these last days he has spoken to us by a Son" (Heb. 1:1–2). There is "something more" that confronts us in the honest, intellectual study of the Scriptures—"a living Word from God which reveals him to man, and in actual fact continues to reveal him as Judge and Savior."[2]

To regard the Bible as divine revelation is a basic presupposition of our approach. To interpret the Scriptures theologically we must recognize the historical principle in revelation; that is, the time and place of the writers in sacred history.[3]

Our aim in interpreting the text is to learn about God—even to be confronted by his living presence. We need to grasp his view of things; to discover eternal principles operative in any given situation, and to see how those "moved by the Holy Spirit" applied them.[4] Beyond that, our task is to view our own situation through this lens and seek to relate or apply those same principles to today's world.

Because God has revealed himself through the writers of Scripture, there is a basis for revelation today through the ministry of the Holy Spirit. "The Spirit's self-revelation of God is not an alternative to biblical study, it is what we expect as we apply ourselves to such study; and biblical study is the chosen means by which the Spirit makes himself known."[5]

Theological concepts in the Bible

Many students of the Bible, including teachers and ministers, have concentrated on a study of particular words. While it is obvious that words are important, words studied in isolation may give misleading impressions of what the Bible teaches about the ideas which those words represent. If we are interested in the study of concepts in Scripture, such as redemption, child-education, the church, etc., it is unreasonable to ground our study primarily on words.[6] How did this habit develop?

It was in the massive work of H. Cremer, *Biblico-Theological Lexicon of New Testament Greek* (1883), that the original impulse was given to theological lexicography (a study of "theological words"). The procedure he used was to point up the similarities and differences between usage of Greek words and the extra-biblical range of meaning. This was followed by the volumes edited by G. Kittel and G. Friedrich, *Theological Dictionary of the New Testament* (1930–73), which treated theological concepts on the basis of words used to express them. The idea here was to study a (Greek) New Testament word in comparison to its use in classical Greek, in its Hebrew equivalent, in the Greek Old Testament, and in the New Testament patterns. The complete results were then applied to the particular text under study.

This approach, however, creates some serious problems.[7] To begin with, it gives a disproportionate emphasis to "word studies," which in practice often means treating words in isolation from their context. The word becomes "a-thing-in-itself." Again, one is in danger of what J. Barr has called "illegitimate totality transfer"—that is, that any one instance of a word contained all possible meanings of a word. This is not possible, for the context of a word will point up a particular sense, as opposed to allowing all possible senses. (Notice the procedure used in the *Amplified Bible*, where often all the meanings of a word are included in parentheses in a specific passage; for example, John 14:16 where the translation of the Greek word *parakletos* "comforter" is given by several English "equivalents.")

Third, one may import a meaning from one text to another, not being aware that the same word is *modified* by a particular phrase or feature in the passage under study. For example, there may be a definite article before a noun, or a preposition may affect the sense. Fourth, if we concentrate upon one word we may miss terms that are semantically related. Suppose we are studying the idea of "servant," reflected in the New Testament word *doulos* "bondservant." We will not want to limit ourselves to this single word; rather we need to look at related words for "servant," such as *oiketes* "house servant" and *misthios* "hired servant." Finally, there is danger in confusing the word for the reality. Rather than studying only the range of meanings of the word *agathos* (good, kind, benificent, etc.) we should include all the Bible has to say about the concept of "goodness." Thus theological thought has characteristic linguistic expression in the word-combination or sentence, not in the word individually or in isolation from related words. Such a statement as "sin is lawlessness" says more about "sin" *hamartia* in a definitive sense than doing a word study of various senses of the word *hamartia* in the Bible. Or to study the theological theme of salvation in Ephesians 1–3 would be of greater value than to do a historical study of the word *sozō* "to save."

Theological aspects of the Bible

Historical exegesis of Scripture demands something beyond discovery of historical data and its significance. It leads us on to theological exegesis. Illustrations of theological patterns through history are available to us within Scripture itself. To read the narrative histories in the Pentateuch—the patriarchal tales, the Exodus, the giving of the Law through Moses at Sinai, and finally entrance into the promised land—is to expose "a faith that the purpose of God must finally be realized, despite all obstinacies of nature and men."[8] The same principle can be seen in the narratives of the book of Acts, along with glimpses in the New Testament letters (see Acts 27:23–26; 2 Cor. 1:8–11).

The story of Joseph clearly illustrates the divine control of history. Having assured his brothers, who had sold him into slavery in Egypt many years earlier, that he bore no grudge against them, he asserted: "for God sent me before you to preserve life.... So it was not you who sent me here, but God" (Gen. 45:5, 8). And again, "As for you, you meant evil against me; but God meant it for good, to bring it about that many people should be kept alive, as they are today" (Gen. 50:20).

In the rest of this section we deal with three issues that continually surface in the attempt to move from historical exegesis to theological application.

(1) One aspect of theological analysis of the text is the question of continuity versus discontinuity between the Old Testament and the New. In our study of the New Testament use of the Old (see chapter four), it was clear that both factors were recognized, although the principle of continuity in the promise/fulfillment theme appeared dominant.

Interest continues in the literature and hermeneutics of the ancient Qumran community near the Dead Sea. There one more witness is added to the variety then current in Judaism. Some have wondered whether Christianity emerged from one of those varied sects in Judaism.[9] Whether or not the final judgment shows more significant differences than similarities, the practices of baptism, a communal meal, certain officers of the community (for example, "overseer"), and the vivid anticipation of the dawning of the kingdom of God, all witness to a kind of continuity between the past and the present.

When we catch a glimpse of the early Church the same issue surfaces. There was, on the one hand, Marcion's view of the "God of wrath" (Old Testament) versus the "God of love" (New Testament). In the present day, the former is often preferred by liberation theologies accompanied by a call for social justice and judgment. J. L. Segundo, an Uruguayan theologian, writes of "the continuing change in our interpretation of the Bible which is dictated by the continuing changes in our present day reality both individual and societal" (a good example of the "hermeneutical circle").[10] While Segundo says "God is love," he also refers to him as "a social God," thus seeing the elements of justice and judgment. Correspondingly, the "God of love" concept is often preferred by the economically privileged upper-class, believing that God has "blessed them" through his love. Yet Marcion's kind of discontinuity is given pause as we observe, against the former case, the message of the book of Hosea ("I will love them freely," 14:4), and, against the latter, the harsh words of John 3:36 ("but the wrath of God rests upon him").

At the same time there is an emphasis on continuity in the early Church. Anticipated by such understanding as noted in Acts 15:6–21, where the words of Amos are applied to Gentiles as well, we observe the language of Justin Martyr (*Dialogue with Trypho,* 47:1–4). He wrote of Jews who "hope on this Christ of ours," while remaining Jews in practice; they must be treated as "of one family and brothers" as long as they do not insist on other Christians following their "rules."

Along with this, the messianic interpretation of the Hebrew Scriptures was an important aspect of continuity. Tertullian, writing of the sacrificial call of Moses' day said, "but behold in the calf's type CHRIST destined *bodily* to suffer"; and of the Exodus, the cloud, and the fire over the Tabernacle he wrote, "He [Christ] led the People out; . . . was Himself the column both of light and of cloud's shade." However we may judge this exegesis, the point argued in the early Church is clear; there is continuity between the old and the new.[11]

(2) In what is currently called "canonical criticism," emphasis is placed on the biblical canon as an entity both stable (a fixed form) and adaptable (continuing to speak to the believing community in successive generations).[12] In this approach, the task of hermeneutics is to interpret the Bible for the community at any particular point in time. The thrust of this hermeneutic is theological—speaking of God, man, and their mutual relationships. Use was made of earlier traditions—whether oral or written—to bear upon a new situation. Interestingly, the use of tradition varied, as can be illustrated from two passages in the prophets' writings.

In the face of divine judgment (namely, the fall of Jerusalem to Nebuchadnezzar), the exiles attempted to draw an analogy with the past in order to gain some comfort, while others were outspoken in saying, "The way of the Lord is not just" (Ezek. 33:17ff.). The former group appealed to Abraham—he was "only one man, yet he got possession of the land; but we are many; the land is surely given us to possess" (v. 24). But the prophet brought a dissenting message from the Lord

(vv. 25–29). Here the use of historical analogy and argument based on what had happened before was counted vain.

In another picture of the exile, the tone is quite different. According to Isa. 51:1–3, the exiles were given a word of comfort and hope (see 40:1–2). Here the prophet told them to "look to the rock from which you were hewn...to Abraham your father," for even as God "blessed him and made him many," so "the Lord will comfort Zion."

What made the difference? It was the historical and theological context. Ezekiel's was a word of judgment for the sin of unfaithfulness to the covenant; Isaiah's was a word of comfort following the judgment. The timing was the crucial thing. A major clue occurs in Isa. 49:8: "In a time of favor I have answered you, in a day of salvation I have helped you." The "time"/"day" was distinct in each case, and the true prophet must know the difference (see Jer. 28:8–9). This means that he must know "the mind of the Lord," for Yahweh had been (in their past) both gracious and severe; sending them into exile and delivering them. God is both free to do whatever he pleases and gracious to those who need his mercy. We cannot assume for today that he will necessarily act in the way that will be the most beneficial and most desirable to us.

Thus we cannot use biblical concepts (traditions, promises, covenants, etc.) in a mechanical fashion. What Kasemann calls "the primary fundamental consideration" of a New Testament hermeneutic is Paul's distinction between letter and spirit. The former refers to Scripture "isolated from the Spirit, and not understood or interpreted according to the intention of the Spirit"; whereas the latter is "the divine power which conveys the righteousness of faith and therefore stands in opposition to the law of the old Mosaic covenant."[13] The distinction between the will of God (for any particular situation) and the letter of Scripture, is a crucial theological question.

Yet the theology (or theological viewpoint) of the materials is frequently obvious (not implying that the meaning or significance is necessarily so). As J. Goldingay has shown in a study of 1 Kings, there is the occurrence of theophany (divine appearance) to the king (3:5ff.; 9:1ff.) and also in the life of the temple cult (11:36; 14:21); the record of God speaking in various forms of utterance (11:37–38; 20:13–14; 22:15–23); and Yahweh's actions in the world (8:12–61).[14] This theology in the tradition makes plain the meaning of the sequences of events. As we ask questions about Solomon's reign, "the event needs the word, of tradition and of prophet, if there is to be an answer." And, in turn, the events give the context for Yahweh's words.

In theological interpretation, both the theology of a particular writer and the larger theology/theologies of the Old and New Testaments should be given attention. If we agree that "all biblical texts are expressive of some aspect of the normative faith of Israel or of the New Testament church,"[15] we will be sensitive to this aspect of Scripture. For the Christian, in particular, the relation between the Old and New Testaments will be crucial, together with the need for a Christological focus. If we are committed to Christ as the Truth, his way of interpreting Scripture needs to become the key to interpretation. A new meaning of history is revealed in Christ, with lasting validity—a view that is in keeping with that of the New Testament writers (see Luke 24:27; Acts 28:23; Rom. 1:1–4; 16:25–26; Eph. 1:9–10, 3:9–10.[16]

(3) A final aspect to think about here is the relation between the living word and the spoken or written word. The Bible begins with a statement of the living, creative word of God; "and God said" (Gen. 1:3ff.). That word brought the world into being, and the multiplicity of living things, including our lives (Gen. 1:26–27).

Then that divine word entered history. God spoke, acted, and revealed himself "in many and various ways." For example, the Old Testament contains many narratives of varying length. The stories of these events contain theological significance. D. Stuart has analyzed three levels of theological meaning in narratives: the "top level" is "that of the whole universal plan of God worked out through his creation"; the "middle level" shows God at work among the people of Israel; the "bottom level" contains many individual narratives which together make up the two levels above.[17]

It is in this "top level" that we see God revealing himself through Christ, for "the Scriptures bear witness to him" (see John 5:37–39). God's universal plan centered in Christ, his redeeming work, and in the reconciling of all things to himself.

The living word "became flesh and dwelt among us" (John 1:14). Reflected in the career of Jesus Christ was the fulfillment of the law of Moses, the prophets, and the psalms (Luke 24:47). He was the goal of the law, the end *telos* toward which it pointed (Rom. 10:4). As G. Fee has put it so colorfully, the Gospels are "One Story, Many Dimensions."[18] Whether one looks at the fourfold story of Jesus in terms of miracle stories, parables, or other narrative materials, one point emerges within all this variety—that "the kingdom of God has drawn near." One can sense the tension between the *already* and the *not yet.* The new age has broken in, yet the consummation is still awaited.

So also in Paul's epistles, the eschatological perspective is clearly evident. While believers have "the first fruits of the Spirit," they yet "groan inwardly...(awaiting) the redemption of (their) bodies" (Rom. 8:23). The universal plan of God for his creation will gain ultimate realization when he reconciles all things to himself, on earth and in heaven, making peace by the redemptive cross of Christ (Col. 1:20).

Thus, in moving from historical to theological exegesis, the principle of the "analogy of faith" (a way of interpreting Scripture since the Reformation by many exegetes), was an approach based on the idea that "Scripture interprets Scripture." In essence, what this meant for the Reformers was that Scripture, rather than church tradition, should be the norm for interpreting Scripture. Kaiser prefers to call it "analogy of [antecedent] Scripture," referring to the idea of using Isaiah to shed light on some text in Romans, and not vice versa![19]

Any theological idea should be weighed against a "theological center" of the biblical materials. Several such organizing centers have been suggested, and it would be dangerous to select any one at the expense of others. For our purposes here we might insist that it should at least be a major emphasis, based upon a careful reading of the whole Bible.[20]

Theological implications and patterns

What are some of the results that could grow out of theological study of the Scriptures? We return for a moment to the characteristics of biblical study in the Reformation period. The sixteenth century leaders replaced allegorical interpretation with exegetical methods that attempted to recover the original (literal) sense of the biblical text. The task of the historical study of Scripture was to launch into theological exegesis. The goal of this, in turn, was to facilitate the proclamation of the gospel of Christ. In this way not only biblical "history" is encountered, but biblical "theology."[21]

An example of this goal being realized is found in the concise (and theological!) statement in Titus 1:1–3. Paul addressed his salutation to his delegate at Crete, Titus, expressing the "hope of eternal life" possessed by God's elect. This life was (1) *promised* by God long ago, and (2) at the suitable time, was *manifested* in the proclamation (of the gospel). Some see this promise in the Bible as early as Gen. 3:15; in any case, it was spoken by the prophets from ancient times (Luke 1:70; Rom. 1:2)—as a promise/fulfillment sequence—and it was manifested in God's Son. Pointedly, the emphasis here is on the "Word" (of God) in the process of revelation and its actualization (in the preaching activity of the apostles).[22]

Not that "the preaching of the Gospel" is an activity of evangelism and nothing beyond it. Rather, it brings the receptive hearer into a place where a truly biblical theology is required, for an individual, for the community of faith, and for the Church. Ultimately it means to declare "the whole counsel [*pasan ton boulen*] of God" (Acts 20:27). B. Ramm sees the main themes of theology as God, man, and Jesus Christ. It is not restricted to lesser concerns, and he states that the literal approach to the meaning of Scripture will be the *control* over the content of theology.[23]

This implies the idea of teaching. The exegetical results of study are the basis for a theology to be communicated to those in the Church. The beginning of Jesus' public ministry was teaching in the synagogues (Mark 1:21; Matt. 4:23, 9:35, 11:1; Luke 4:15), and "with every word He brought His hearers into direct confrontation with the will of God as it is revealed in His Word and as it is constantly revealed in history."[24] This was based upon examples in the Hebrew Scriptures, where the statutes and the ordinances were taught to Israel, and were to be taught to succeeding generations "that they may live" (Deut. 4:1, 10). Jesus brought his hearers into that same situation—a communication of the will of God and a call to order life in view of the teaching (Matt. 22:34–40, 19:16–22).

The early Church continued this pattern. Matthew's gospel concludes with the command to "make disciples...teaching them to observe all things I have commanded you" (Matt. 28:19–20); the earliest converts in Jerusalem "devoted themselves to the apostles' teaching" (Acts 2:42); the apostles continued this function both publicly (4:2) and within the context of the community (6:4). In the wider world, the leading figures (Barnabas, Paul, and others) carried on teaching in Antioch (11:26, 13:1), Paphos (13:12), Corinth (18:11), Apollos in Ephesus (18:25), and Paul again in Rome (28:31). Particularly in Paul's career, teaching *didaskein* refers to the instruction given to the communities of believers at the time of their founding (2 Thess. 2:15, Col. 2:7, Eph. 4:21).[25] It is noteworthy that Paul's teaching is based on the model given by Jesus (Gal. 5:14, Rom. 13:8–10).

Another point worth noting here is the scope of theological study and communication. R. B. Y. Scott calls us to know the Bible first as a historical document—get to know "the biblical world." We can better understand Amos if we know the circumstances and religious development in his background. Then we need to interpret theologically—to see "the place and importance of the passage in question in the religious thought of the Bible as a whole." All this is of first importance for Christian thought in the present in terms of the great themes of Scripture. Certain crucial religious convictions are expressed in characteristic ways, and this "biblical theology" is "the essential basis of any religious thought which can call itself Christian."[26]

This means that exegetical work must maintain a close tie with the discipline of theology, the latter being the formulation of Christian teaching in any particular age or setting. By this means we can prevent exegesis being done in isolation or detachment from the issues of life. We need to relate theology to the particular historical situation in which people confront problems and ask "what word there is from the Lord" to clarify, understand, and find a solution to the problems.[27] To observe how the biblical writers understood the nature of God and his relations to people, and how they applied those insights to their own historical situation, ought to give a basis for addressing the present situation.

Care needs to be exercised, however, in necessarily equating the original significance of a biblical text or principle with its current significance. Marshall has reminded us to ask whether any particular scriptural text is universal in application.[28] The answer may well be found as we study the text or principle in its original context. Yet, granted that there is a difference between the biblical writings and ourselves in culture, time, language, etc., the point should not be overstressed. More than one writer today has expressed "the ring of truth" which the Bible often has for modern people. It continues not only as "the Word of God" but as a message that probes, analyzes, and prescribes for the deep needs of the human being. To the believing heart "it works" (1 Thess. 2:13).

Particularly with biblical commands we sense this tension

of appropriateness. How shall we today apply such commands as these?: "Go up to the hills and bring wood and build the house" (Hag. 1:8); "Bring the full tithes into the storehouse" (Mal. 3:10); "Let every person be subject to the governing authorities" (Rom. 13:1); "No longer drink water, but use a little wine for the sake of your stomach and your frequent ailments" (1 Tim. 5:23). Such commands appear quite different in form and nature from the following, even for the present day: "You shall love the Lord your God with all your heart, and with all your soul, and with all your might" (Deut. 6:4); "Seek the Lord and live" (Amos 5:6); "Bear one another's burdens" (Gal. 6:2); "Continue steadfastly in prayer" (Col. 4:2).

What makes the difference in our response to these two sets of commands, both of which are "biblical"? In the former we may well see differences from our own situation in the very historical situation itself, or in the existing conditions of the group addressed, or in the cultural habits. Further, we may see a theological difference—some of these words were addressed to Israel, not to the Church. Or there may simply be the general sense of the inappropriateness of such things for today's world or situation. The latter group, on the other hand, will probably ring true no matter when or where we are within the Christian spectrum. To love the Lord and seek him, and to share the burdens of our fellows— these appear to be commands quite in keeping with timeless application.

Does this imply that much of Scripture no longer has meaning or application to the life of the Church? Are we delivered from much of its detail in practice, and shall we just emphasize attitudes of love, sympathy, etc.? For some, indeed, that has become so in theory and, with many more, in practice. Further, what about issues on which the Bible says nothing specific? We are not told what vocation to follow, what marriage partner to choose, or what recreational pursuits to enjoy.

(1) There is need to regard the Bible as "the Word of God"

and authoritative for the life of the people of God at any time in their history. We are not free to choose whether to hear the Scriptures; they come to us as words able to lead us to salvation and call us to obedience. In both Old and New Testaments there is the sense of the divine authority of the message (Deut. 11:1, Matt. 5:19–20, Heb. 2:1–4, Rev. 22:18–19). The truth-value of Scripture is an important factor to be retained in our thinking and it is the basis of our sanctification (Ps. 119:9–11, 160; John 17:17).

(2) There is need for contemporary expressions of the doctrinal concepts of the Bible. Theology is essentially a human attempt to express the teachings of Scripture. It is thus subject to that same tentativeness and need for refinement characteristic of any human system of thought. It is Scripture, not our explanation of it, that is "the enduring Word of God." One needs to stay "genuinely open to the message of Scripture *before, during,* and *after* one molds and formulates it into an organized structure," remembering that "now we see in a mirror dimly"; that we know only "in part," not fully (1 Cor. 13:12).[29] Doctrinal concepts should be expressed in contemporary terms while remaining true to the biblical teachings. This will protect against heretical systems, on the one hand and against rationalism on the other. Whether we deal with the doctrine of the Trinity, salvation by grace, heaven, or the Second Coming of Christ—these need to be handled with biblically based exegesis and theology, yet expressed in contemporary language and related to the understanding of the era through systematic theology and exposition. That hearers or readers understand the message is crucial. If this requires reformulation, that aim must be clearly realized. To do so will, in turn, allow the authority of Scripture for the present day to be sensed.

(3) There is need to discover enduring principles in the Scriptures. As we have noted, many passages may appear ancient and unrelated to today's needs. How may this be remedied? Notice Paul's question addressed to the text of Deut. 25:4 ("You shall not muzzle an ox when it treads out

the grain."): "Is it for oxen that God is concerned? Does he not speak entirely for our sake? It was written for our sake" (1 Cor. 9:9–10). That particular text, literally interpreted and applied, has little or no relevance for an apostle in need of financial support, or even for the urban Corinthians. So Paul drew a higher sense from it.[30] The principle was God's care for his creatures (whether oxen or apostles), and the contemporary application, therefore, was that Christian workers were to be supported by those in whose interest they were doing their work. Without denying the literal sense of the passage, Paul moves the passage into a new situation and sees a new sense for new needs. But notice the close connections. Both oxen and Christian workers are God's creatures; God cares for all his creatures.

How would one preach from Nehemiah 6, relating it to the present? One suggestion is that one learns "how godly men handle personal attacks while attempting a ministry for God."[31] And what about Rom. 13:1? Is it appropriate under all circumstances? What about for German Christians in 1939 under Hitler's regime or for North American Christians in Nebraska who are prohibited by the authorities from operating an uncertified private school in the 1980s? Are they both commanded to "be subject to the governing authorities"? To derive a "yes" answer from Romans 13 is questionable.

Paul's letters generally addressed specific needs in his churches. He was writing for that situation, not necessarily for every situation. What was his intent for them as a community of believers? Was it not that they might continue to live and witness? What would civil disobedience mean against the might of Rome? The Christian community was small and unrecognized by the Roman government. Any "rebellion" was out of the question: "for he does not bear the sword in vain" (Rom. 13:4). There was a better, if less efficient way, to win out. (Much the same approach was taken to the problem of slavery; for example, Col. 3:22–4:1.) If the circumstances had been different, Paul's answer may well have been different too. If there are legitimate ways to "protest," each situation is clearly a new one. The Israelites leaving Egypt, the Jerusalemites standing against the threats of Sennacherib of Assyria, the restoration leaders of Judah "protesting" for their rights to King Darius of Persia, or Paul protesting the ruling of the Sanhedrin against him and appealing to his "rights" as a Roman citizen—all these incidents hardly fit with the often-repeated idea of a kind of passive subjection to authority.

(4) There is need to carry over whatever we can from the teachings and commands of Scripture. God gave his Word for the ultimate good of his people (Rom. 15:4; 1 Cor. 10:11; 2 Tim. 3:16–17). Is it possible that some of our hermeneutical dilemmas arise due to changes in our mindset and our ways of relating to life? We have noted earlier the need to let the Scriptures speak to us to bring about changes in attitudes we have come to hold. Often subtly "the cares of the world, and the delight in riches, and the desire for other things, enter in and choke the word, and it proves unfruitful" (Mark 4:19). The danger of being "conformed to this world" calls for "the renewal of the mind" in order to demonstrate the will of God (Rom. 12:2).

Placing these issues in the perspective of our own position, we also would emphasize the great truths of Scripture that are enduring. First, God is Creator and Redeemer, and he cares for his people. The Bible is thus given for the ultimate good of his people. Second, whatever is stated as a command, directive, or principle for God's people *generally* should be considered for application to ourselves. (This means, negatively, that such things given to specific people may not be meant for all.) If the words are not able to be carried over in the same way in which they were originally intended, then we must return to the approach described in the previous section on "enduring principles." Third, we may carry out a specific command, directive, or principle apart from the particular circumstances with which it was first connected. For example, we may "preach the gospel" by means of radio or television, although that was obviously not the way the early Christians carried out the command. Finally, the spirit and power of our responses need to be in the love of Christ and in the energy of the Holy Spirit. To do what we do in the wrong spirit and with fleshly energy may be "to win a battle, but lose the war."

(5) There is need for balance in our theological exegesis and application of biblical teaching. Walking a tightrope is no mean accomplishment, but life often calls for such an endeavor. Chasms of all kinds must be crossed if we are to survive unscathed. (Most of us carry signs of many bumps and bruises.)

First, we need balance between reading the Bible as a historical/theological book and a devotional book. There is the Bible for information and the Bible for power—and every Christian needs to have these "two Bibles." This does not necessarily mean reading different parts of the Bible in each case; for example, 2 Samuel as opposed to the Psalms. One can read the same text in the two ways (for example, Genesis 12–25); as a historical narrative, noting the various details, or as a record of God's gracious covenant with his servant Abraham (who was called "the Friend of God"). One reading no less than the other calls for an alert mind, a humble, teachable spirit, and a prayer for the guidance of the Holy Spirit, who "leads us into all the truth."

Second, we need balance between prayer and action. Each is right in its own place, but one will not do as a substitute for the other. Take these examples in the Book of Nehemiah: "Hear, O our God, for we are despised. . . . So we built the wall. . . . And we prayed to our God, and set a guard as a protection against them day and night. . . . Remember the Lord, who is great and terrible, and fight against them" (Neh. 4:4–6, 9, 14). Notice in each case the prayer or the appeal to God, followed by action: "Hear, O our God. . . . so we built"; "And we prayed . . . and set a guard"; "Remember the Lord . . . and fight." Our call to God (that is, prayer) is balanced by his call to us (that is, to take action). Additional examples will be found in the cases of Joshua (Josh. 5:13–15),

Isaiah (Isa. 6:5–9), and our Lord himself, who prayed before many major crises (Luke 5:12–13, 22:41–44, followed by his death; see Heb. 5:7–10).

Third, we need balance between dependence on the Holy Spirit and the exercise of our gifts. What God has committed to us in terms of gifts he expects us to use in his service. Recall Paul's instructions: "Having gifts that differ according to the grace given to us, let us use them" (Rom. 12:6). Peter counsels the same advice: "As each has received a gift, employ it for one another" (1 Pet. 4:10). The parables of Jesus are frequent reminders of stewards or servants who failed to use (or use rightly) the resources given them by their master. On the other hand, those who did use their resources wisely and well were described as "good and faithful servants," receiving the master's, "Well done!"

CHAPTER ELEVEN

Models of Interpreting Scripture

WE HAVE ARRIVED at a point which calls for some specific models of exegesis involving various kinds of biblical texts. When one studies any biblical text, is it as text or as Scripture?[1] The former may result in some psychological influence on the work of the theologian. Exegesis of the text as "text" may well result also in a critical examination of the status quo of the Christian community. Historically this has often occurred in times of important reform in the Church. This, in turn, has led to further evaluation of the results of exegesis.

Yet it is the text as Scripture that ought to provide a normative standard, showing the authoritativeness of the texts for the life of the Church. In chapter two we have discussed the question of the authority of the Bible. A twofold sense emerged in that the Bible claims a "Word of God" character, thus possessing an authoritative quality; it has also functional authority, as it is applied to the life of the Church.

Much of what we read in the Bible is "pre-scriptive" in character. It is a word meant to order one's thinking about God, one's interpretation of self and the world, or the direction of life for individual and community. These texts may be basically theological, or they may contain moral and ethical prescriptions. On the other hand, there is much in the Bible which is descriptive; for example, narrative history or poetic reflections. To what extent, if at all, is such material normative for individual or community? We may find normativeness either in theological or moral principles common to all cultures, or in a parallel historical situation which lends a strong degree of identification between text and reader. Even unconsciously such texts have a way of shaping our religious outlook,[2] if not contributing to our own formulation of theological insights. To the extent that the Bible in itself is authoritative, these influences will be salutary.

Historical narrative (1 Kings 21)

The story of Naboth's vineyard has long stood as an example of a greedy king wanting to acquire a piece of property, although this meant a violation of property rights. Was he any better (or worse) than Esau, "Who sold his birthright for a single meal" (Heb. 12:16)? Is this what the story was and is meant to teach? Do we have here an individualistic moral narrative? Or are there larger issues involved, and how may we get at them?[3]

Two factors are important in interpreting this passage: (1) the historical setting of the Ahab/Elijah story in the context of 1 Kings, and (2) the sociological setting in the world of ninth century Israel.

Ahab had succeeded his father, Omri, as king of Israel, reigning ca. 869–850 B.C. He married Jezebel, daughter of Ethbaal, king of the Sidonians (Phoenicia). Through this union the worship of the Phoenician god Ba'al was fostered in Israel. This is one of the causes of the conflict between Ahab and the prophet Elijah. Among the military engagements of Ahab's reign were the battles against Ben-hadad of Syria (1 Kings 20, 22) and his participation in the battle of Qarqar (853 B.C.) against Shalmanezer III of Assyria. (The latter is mentioned only in an Assyrian inscription; it does not appear in 1 Kings.)[4] In 1 Kings 17–22, much attention is given to the king's encounters with Elijah—the contest with the prophets of Ba'al on Mt. Carmel (chap. 18) and the murder of Naboth (chap. 21). In each of these passages Ahab expressed his estimate of Elijah as "troubler of Israel" (18:17) and "my enemy" (21:20).

Certain historical notes within the passage may be helpful to exegesis. Naboth's vineyard in Jezreel was near Ahab's palace (v. 1). This was probably a summer residence, as the king's main residence was in Samaria. The title "king of Samaria" may reflect the center of power in the house of Omri.[5] The socio-economic position of Naboth was probably among the landed nobility of Jezreel (see vv. 8, 12). In the tradition of the Torah, two witnesses were brought against Naboth (Deut. 17:6).

With regard to the sociological setting of the text, notice the agrarian culture, indicated by an emphasis on land and rights of property. Land in Israel was related to the covenant. It was for Naboth "the inheritance of my fathers" (v. 3), the sale of which was forbidden by law (Lev. 25:23, Num. 36:7). The land belonged to the Lord, and was held in trust by families within each tribe. Jezebel's question,[6] "Do you now govern Israel?" (v. 7) is one of the keys to interpretation of the passage. The pronoun "you" occurs first in the Hebrew text for the sake of emphasis; the statement assumes the royal prerogative.

A comment by J. Robinson appears to pinpoint the matter.[7] "Ahab's style of ruling raised the fundamental issue of the relationship of the king to the law. The whole pattern of Israel's life as the covenant people was directed by laws and customs which declared how God would have the people live. *Ahab determined to change this*" (italics mine). Thus a clash developed between God's authority (through the covenant) and the king's authority. Historically, Israel had affirmed that "God is king" (rather than "the king is god").

The charge mounted against Naboth was that he "cursed God and the king" (v. 13). He had actually challenged the religious power of the state. Ahab and Jezebel became threatened because the covenant with Yahweh was at stake. Elijah's role (vv. 17ff.) was not to rebuke Ahab for some personal sin such as greed but to call the king to affirm and obey the covenant given through Moses.[8] The issue was clear; the king had come close to usurping the place of God. Thus the emphasis of the passage is a major theological theme, and in making use of the text for teaching, or as a sermon text, this should be clearly focused.

It is well to realize that narrative material ought to be interpreted as a whole, and within its historical and cultural framework. Basically, as a story, it is a unit of material, intended to make a particular point; that is, to carry a basic message from author to reader. The details within the narrative contribute to this main point. As one has said, "In the final analysis, God is the hero of all biblical narratives."

Further, biblical narratives are descriptive rather than normative. They tell what happened to someone else, not what I, as reader, ought to do. This does not mean that moral precepts ("thou shalt not steal") or implicit messages (it is wrong to steal) may not lie behind the narratives. But we need to read them as revelations of God's activities within the sphere of human life, and then turn to directive material in the Bible to gain moral and ethical norms for living.

For teaching or homiletical purposes the following outline may be suggested:

Theme: Who Is In Charge?

(1) Ahab's desire to acquire property (vv. 1–4).
(2) Jezebel's solution to the problem (vv. 5–7).
(3) Naboth's trial and death (vv. 8–14).
(4) Ahab's seizure of the property (vv. 15–16).
(5) Elijah's message of judgment (vv. 17–24).
(6) Ahab's repentance (vv. 25–29).

Conclusion: God is in charge.

Prophetic announcement (Isaiah 7:14)

There is seemingly endless fascination among Bible readers with the subject of "prophecy." Often that term implies a predictive kind of writing; especially texts that seem to deal with the coming of the end of the world. Disagreements among expositors and confusion among average readers apparently reduce the task to hopeless proportions.

Once again good tools can be a help just in getting started. Read, for example, B. Ramm's discussion in his *Protestant Biblical Interpretation* (chapter X) on "The Interpretation of Prophecy"; or, D. Stuart's "The Prophets—Enforcing the Covenant in Israel" (chapter 10), in *How to Read the Bible for All Its Worth*. These are "starters", and there are other good sources suggested in both these books.

Can we interpret prophetic books and texts by our usual methods of interpretation (such as noted in chapters seven to ten above)? Or do we need some "special approach" to prophecy? While we would say that our basic approach would be the same in the book of Genesis or the gospel of Mark, there is an important factor that needs to be observed: The prophets spoke *to* us rather than *about* us. They had a word from God for eighth century Israel (as Amos) or for first century Christians (as John in his Apocalypse/Revelation). We should exercise great caution against simply carrying over their teachings in direct fashion to ourselves today.

We could ask this question another way. Did the message of the prophets have more than a single meaning? (Review the section on *sensus plenior* in chapter four above.) The answer to this question in relation to the Old Testament ought to be derived from the New Testament use of the Old. There is an important reason for this. As a New Testament writer interpreted an Old Testament prophecy in a way different from the natural sense of the message originally given by the prophet, he was writing (interpreting) by the inspiration of the Holy Spirit. As has often been noted, we today may be blessed by the *illumination* of the Holy Spirit, but are not inspired as they were. For example, in interpreting Jer. 31:31–34, would one apply it to non-Israelites? Now see Heb. 8:7–13. Or, when interpreting Joel 2:28–32, would one understand it to be fulfilled before "the day of the Lord"? Now see Acts 2:14–21. Or, when interpreting Amos 9:11–15, would one apply it to all nations? Compare Acts 15:14–18.

To be more specific, let us examine a specific text in the Old Testament—the dramatic words of the prophet Isaiah to King Ahaz of Judah—Isa. 7:14. Few single texts in the Bible have raised such a storm in interpretation as this. The controversy is centered on the meaning and the implications of the word *almah*. Should it be translated as "young woman," "maiden," or "virgin"? A purely lexical observation at the outset will not be decisive. It comes from a Hebrew root *a.l.m.*, meaning "to conceal." A survey of uses of the noun in the Old Testament shows the following:[9]

> Gen. 24:43—"maiden" NASB, "young woman" RSV;
> Exod. 2:8—"girl" NASB, "girl" RSV;
> Prov. 30:19—"maid" NASB, "young woman" RSV;
> Song 1:3, 6:8—"maidens" NASB, "maidens" RSV.

Is the primary emphasis on the age of the woman or on her marital/biological state? And beyond this, of course, is the question arising from the use of the word within the context of Isa. 7:14? For many, at least, the controversy is more theological than semantic.

The context is the story of the dilemma of King Ahaz of Judah (Isa. 7:1–24). He was threatened by a military attack from Israel and Syria (v. 1). Isaiah the prophet was sent to calm his fears (vv. 3–4). When Ahaz refused to ask the Lord for a sign of deliverance from his adversaries (vv. 10–12), he was given a sign by the Lord (vv. 14–19). A child would be born, and would be a sign that God would be with the nation of Judah ("Emmanuel"). Yet, because of his unbelief, the king and his people would experience judgment. The historical sources for the story are found in 2 Kings 16 and 2 Chronicles 28. In 2 Kin. 16:5, the invaders could not conquer Ahaz. In 2 Chron. 28:5 he was defeated and many of his people taken captive to Damascus. It appears Isa. 7:1 describes the situation given in 2 Kings.[10]

How would the birth of a child be a "sign" to Ahaz? Attention should be given to the word "sign" as used in the Scriptures. J. A. Motyer has described two distinct senses: (1) a sign is a way of promoting some action or reaction in the immediate present (see Exod. 4:8–9; Deuteronomy 13, and Isa. 7:11, 14); (2) something designed to follow a series of events, to confirm them as acts of God, thus fixing a stated interpretation on them (see Exod. 3:12).[11] He argues for the second sense, based upon the facts that Ahaz had for making an immediate decision about what to do; all he had to work with in the present was the word from God through Isaiah. E. J. Young approves a third sense; a "sign" may be a miracle (Exod. 4:8–9; 7:8–13; Isa. 38:7).[12] Clements takes "sign" as something vested with special divine meaning and significance and links it to the name borne by the child, rather than any circumstances surrounding the birth.[13]

On the one hand, the prediction in v. 14 is deeply involved in the current situation. We read in vv. 15–16 of what appears to be a relatively near time for the birth of the child. Further in Isa. 8:1–4, similar language is tied in with the child born to Isaiah's wife, and he would also be a "sign" of the downfall of the enemies of Judah.

Yet the context of Isaiah 7–11 gives evidence of greater scope to the prophecy of 7:14. A comparison of the following texts is instructive: (1) 7:1–17 with 9:8–10:4; (2) 7:18–8:8 with 10:5–15; (3) 8:9–22 with 10:16–34; and (4) 9:1–7 with 11:1–16. This moves from decision, to judgment, to remnant, to a glorious hope. Seen in this light, Isaiah 7 shows both divine promises given and abrogated (due to unbelief), which are to be fulfilled at a later time.[14] Who could fulfill the ultimate sense? Who would "Emmanuel" be?

A Christian response is given in Matt. 1:18–25. Matthew gives special emphasis to the passage by citing the LXX text, in which *almah* is rendered by the Greek word *parthenos* "virgin." This was truly a "sign," for "that which is conceived in her is of the Holy Spirit" (1:20). J. Calvin commented that "Emmanuel" "cannot apply to a man who is not God."[15]

Thus, first of all, a prophet spoke to his own day. There was a definite message of promise to Ahaz and the house of David. Yet he refused to accept the word, choosing rather to call on Assyria than to accept divine deliverance in another form. But the whole context points to a larger and loftier solution, as the language of Isa. 9:6–7 and 11:1–3 seems to say. There would be a greater monarch to sit on David's throne (Luke 1:32–33).

Miracle story (Matthew 8:5–13)

This is a story, found also in Luke 7:1–10, of a centurion who besought Jesus to heal his servant, who was lying paralyzed at home. Jesus marvelled at his faith, commended him highly, and granted the healing (at his word) from a distance. In addition to a comparison with the Lukan narrative there is also another story of a Gentile approaching Jesus in Matt. 15:21–28.[16]

The gospel of Mark does not contain this story, so scholars normally refer to it as "Q" material (from German *Quelle*, meaning "source"). While the accounts in Matthew and Luke are similar, they are not equivalent. The closest verbal similarity is in the dialogue material (compare Matt. 8b–10 with Luke 7:6b, 7b–9), a feature common to the synoptic Gospels. Also, the words in Matt. 8:11–12 are used by Luke in another context (see Luke 13:28–29). Further, Matthew's account is not just a "miracle" narrative; he lays emphasis on Jesus' sayings regarding authority and faith.

In the face of these characteristics, it is well to recall that the evangelists did not feel bound to speak with a single voice. They apparently felt free to omit or recount details, or to arrange material in various patterns. (What their motives may have been can be responded to only with guesswork.)[17] When we read the two accounts we see Matthew stressing faith, while Luke is stressing humility. Matthew may have used omission to clarify his emphasis on the faith of the Gentile.

Now we may turn to a commentary-oriented exegesis of the passage. This is another approach or model for explaining a passage.

(V. 5) Capernaum was the center of Jesus' ministry in Galilee (see Matt. 4:13 and Mark 2:1, where Jesus was "at home"). It was a key city in the first century. In addition to the Roman centurion, a high-ranking official (John 4:46), as well as the tax-officer Levi (Matt. 9:9) lived there. The centurion was a non-commissioned officer of Herod's army, a commander of (usually) 100 men, and a counterpart to his Roman army officer. Centurions were known for their dependability and bravery in battle. Matthew lays emphasis on his gentile origins; Luke on his character.

(V. 6) How shall we translate *kyrios* "lord" and also *pais* "servant" or "child"? The former term, which can be rendered "Sir" (polite address) or "Lord" (for superiors), appears to acknowledge the superiority of Jesus; the latter is best taken as "servant" due to the tenor of the story (see v. 9).[18]

(V. 7) Literally, Jesus replied, "I [emphatic] coming will heal him." There is a problem of punctuation here. Is it an assurance or a question? Probably the latter, as if to say, "Do you want me, a Jew, to come to your (gentile) house and heal him?" Compare v. 10 and vv. 11–12 for emphasis.

(V. 8) Why is the title "Lord" repeated? The centurion declares himself "not worthy" (a moral insufficiency; see Matt. 3:11 and 1 Cor. 15:9; compare also the woman's use of "dogs" in another gentile incident, Matt. 15:27). He was willing to trust Jesus' word for the healing.[19]

(V. 9) What did the centurion think about Jesus by his analogy of "authority"? Rather, what do his words mean? Is it a comparison, or contrast with Jesus? P. A. Micklem suggested three ideas:[20] (a) he is subordinate—Jesus is supreme; (b) if he can command—how much more can Jesus; (c) his authority is exercised through others—Jesus simply has to speak a word. (Greek students will want to give attention to the opening words, *kai gar ego*.)

(V. 10) Only here and in Mark 6:6 do we read that Jesus "marvelled" (here at belief, there at unbelief). The word "truly" (literally *amen*) occurs thirty times in Matthew and in the Gospels at the beginning of some solemn saying, "to show that as such they are reliable and true."[21] Notice the high commendation of this gentile's faith in Jesus' power to heal ("with no-one in Israel").

(Vv. 11–12) Due to these words being formed in another

setting in Luke (see 13:28–29), some take them as Matthew's own arrangement, adding to the story some words of Jesus, to emphasize the coming in of the Gentiles (who believe) and the exclusion of "the sons of the kingdom" (who disbelieve). This is the language of the Prophet (see Matt. 10:15; 12:36).

(V. 13) Compare Matt. 15:27. In both cases a strong emphasis on faith (by a gentile seeker). Healing takes place at the utterance of the authoritative words of Jesus.

Based on the exegetical data, what theological themes characterize the passage? Notice the following: (1) the authority and compassion of Jesus; (2) the humility and faith of the centurion; (3) the relation of faith to healing; (4) the relation of faith to destiny; and (5) the nature of the two destinies. These emphases are largely extensions of Old Testament teachings; others occur in the intertestamental literature. The books of Isaiah, Enoch, and the Psalms of Solomon contain many precedents.

Gospel narrative (Matthew 22:34–40)

What has already been noted concerning the New Testament use of the Old may be further illustrated by a study of one of the central narrative texts in the gospel—the question about "the great commandment of the law."[22] Particularly it may be seen by some striking contrast with the account in Mark 12:28–34. Notice some of the contrasts between the two:

Matt. 22:34–40	Mark 12:28–34
(1) a lawyer *(nomikos)*	(1) a scribe *(grammateus)*
(2) "the great commandment" in the law?	(2) "the first of all?"
(3) (no response from lawyer)	(3) God is one; and love for God and neighbor
	(4) lower estimate of offerings and sacrifices

Matthew's account lays heavier emphasis on the *Jewish* aspects: a lawyer, the law, and the dependence of the Law and the

Prophets on these two commandments, thus stressing the authority of the Old Testament and Jesus' approach to it.[23] Mark's account makes the scribe's query "more like a philosophical question concerning the fundamental principles for a good life," rather than a dispute about the relative importance of the Torah's commands. Further, the brief rule about the love of God and the love of one's neighbors is more like the Hellenistic approach to life than it is rabbinic (this combination of Deut. 6:5 and Lev. 19:18 seems to be absent from rabbinic writings).

Matthew's narrative, then, is a carefully worded example of how Jesus and the early Church approached the Scriptures; it is "a very carefully formulated hermeneutic program."[24] Here the lawyer's question is an exegetical problem—how does one determine the order of precedence of statements in the Scriptures? By calling Deut. 6:4–5 "the great and first commandment," Jesus then raises Lev. 19:18 to the rank of "the second." The latter is "like" the former—it deals with the subject of love as well. Finally, Jesus' reference to "all the Law and the Prophets" may include what are called "the writings" as well (see Luke 24:27, 44), thus giving an approach to the whole of the Old Testament.

Rabbinic rules of interpretation may be seen in Jesus' hermeneutics. For example, the rule of Hillel which justified "constructing a family from two scriptural texts" is reflected in vv. 37–40. Again, the rule that two verses containing the same word should be kept together, is seen here by use of the two verses containing the word "love."

Summing up, we see the hermeneutics of the passage to be as follows: (a) The books of the Old Testament (that is, "the Law and the Prophets") remain valid; thus God's people must continue to hear them. (b) The threefold command to love God is basic for one's living—not simply as a "principle" but as a "vision." (c) Loving and serving God is joined to loving and serving one's fellowman. A passage such as this can be basic in observing Jesus' method of teaching (see v. 36, "Teacher") in the Gospels, especially in Matthew. In relation to the first summary principle above, compare the material in Matt. 5:17–48. There is an emphasis on "hearing" the commandments (vv. 21, 27, 33, 38, 43, "you have heard"). Jesus taught that the Law was to be heard and obeyed (see Matt. 23:2, 3a). But here he gives a radical reinterpretation. Not simply the external acts but the attitude was crucial; you are to love God and to love your neighbor. How can one's righteousness exceed that of the scribes and Pharisees (v. 20)?—once again, by love; a love that is "with all your heart, and with all your soul, and with all your mind."

As a final comparison with Matthew's account (22:34–40), it will be instructive to observe Luke's material. He placed the story earlier (Luke 10:25–28) and as a response to a question about inheriting eternal life. Following this, however, is probably the most popular story in Luke's gospel, the Good Samaritan (10:29–37). It is a magnificent illustration of the practice of the neighbor principle; that is, what one ought to do in the face of the principle.

Parable (Luke 18:9–14)

This pericope is made up of three well-marked divisions: the setting/occasion (v. 9); the story (vv. 10–13); and the principle (v. 14). At the outset we may inquire about the audience for the parable and its purpose. Rather than being an instruction on how to pray (although the point of humility is stressed), it was directed against certain unnamed opponents of Jesus to show them the mercy and pity of God toward the humble and despised. Jeremias contends that it is addressed to the Pharisees, a conclusion confirmed by the content of the parable.[25]

(V. 9) The word "that" (Greek *hoti*) might better be translated "because" (see 2 Cor. 1:9 where people who actually "trusted in themselves" are contrasted with those who "trusted in God"), thus emphasizing the reason rather than the content of their self-confidence.[26] To be "righteous" meant "practicing conduct that makes one acceptable to God."

(V. 10) The hours of prayer were about 9:00 A.M. and 3:00 P.M. during the times of the morning and evening sacrifices in the Temple (see Exod. 30:7–8; Luke 1:10; and Acts 3:1). Sharp contrast with respect to observing the Torah is given by a Pharisee and a tax collector; further, the former despised the latter for his associations with "unclean" people and things.

(V. 11) The expression "with himself" is difficult with regard to translation and syntax—that is, to what does it relate: to standing or to prayer? J. Jeremias and I. H. Marshall favor the former ("he took up a prominent position and uttered this prayer" or "taking his stand, prayed"). J. M. Creed adopts the latter: "he prayed with himself" (see also RSV).[27] The Pharisee had fulfilled the demands of the Law, thus his prayer is genuine, though it may sound ostentatious to later readers.[28]

(V. 12) The Pharisee did more than the Law demanded. According to Lev. 16:29 and 23:27, a yearly fast was prescribed (on the Day of Atonement); the Pharisees were practicing it every Monday and Thursday. According to Deut. 14:22–23, a tithe was to be paid on produce from the field and the firstlings of herd and flock; the Pharisees were tithing on all their income, not only their possessions.

(V. 13) Tax collectors contracted to collect taxes for the state, and made private profit out of the collections. People considered them as robbers (compare "unjust," in v. 11, meaning a "swindler") and all respectable people avoided them. Luke gives several other examples of publicans (3:12, 5:29–31 and 19:1–10; especially 19:8, "if I have defrauded anyone of anything"!). He beat his breast: "more accurately, the heart, as the seat of sin, is an expression of the deepest contrition" (Jeremias). He confessed his state as "the sinner" and called upon God for mercy (see Ps. 51:1).

(V. 14) The sense of the participle is "having been [and going on his way] justified." He had been declared acquitted by God. (This is the only use of the verb in the Gospels in the "Pauline" sense.) A remarkable first century A.D. Jewish prayer is found in 2 Esdras 12:7ff.: "O Sovereign Lord, if I have found favor in thy sight, and if I have been accounted righteous before thee beyond many others, and if my prayer has indeed come up before thy face." It would be shocking to the hearers of this parable that God would listen to the prayer of a publican! The closing statement in v. 14 (and see Luke 14:11, Matt. 23:12) is to be considered, not as a pithy axiom alone but as referring to God's eschatological judgment—the humbling of the proud and the exalting of the humble in the Last Day.[29]

What is the point of the parable? Is it to condemn Pharisees, to praise tax collectors, or to teach about humility and confession of sin? Is it a parable about how to pray or about the nature of God who justifies the ungodly? The last question will remind us of the criticisms of an "objective" view of the parable leveled by W. Wink.[30] He alerts us as to how the modern reader has "actually turned it into its opposite," by identifying with the tax collector (strangely, "the good guy" as against "the bad guy"). He calls the reader to take the two men as "dual aspects of a single alienating structure," to see ourselves as making *both* responses, and "to transcend both by their reconciliation under the justifying love of God." What he has done, while possibly overstating the case, is to show modern listeners (with a long Christian tradition), that the impact of the story is quite different from that in the original setting.[31]

This is a fine example of how our mindset, our horizon, must be corrected in order to merge with that of the writer/text of Scripture. It is a call both to recover the original sense of the text and to bring a legitimate application into the present.

Theological exhortation (Hebrews 4:12)

If the reader wonders why this verse is cited in isolation (and, as such, seems only implicitly an "exhortation"), it is due to the fact that the text is so often quoted or alluded to in isolation! It is one of the favorite texts to describe the character of "the Word of God" or to argue for the nature of man as composed of "soul and spirit." This study is a call not only to give a careful exegesis of the details of a single verse but to consider the context in which it is found (particularly Heb. 1:1–4:13).

Certainly the main subject of the verse itself is found in its opening phrase "the word of God." Thus it is legitimate to ask what the writer means by "the word of God"? The immediate context is vv. 11–13, where we have an exhortation in the opening verse, the basis for it in v. 12, and the logic of it made explicit in v. 13. It might be phrased, "Strive"—"because"—("and this means everyone!"). Whoever wants to enter "that rest" (v. 11; see 3:11, 18–19; 4:1, 3, 5, 8–10) must strive to do so; meaning obeying by faith the Word of God (see 3:7, 15, 19; 4:2, 3, 6, 7). The two elements are united by Westcott in his comment, "The necessity of earnest effort lies in the character of the divine revelation."[32] Within the discussion, the writer gives an example of one who "entered in" (4:14) and an example of some who did not (4:2).

That there is danger in failing to heed the exhortation of v. 11 is made clear in several previous statements: (a) those who transgressed and disobeyed the Word (2:1–2); (b) those in the wilderness (3:7–11); (c) those who hear the Word now (3:12–15); (d) the present opportunity (4:1). Notice the hortatory phrases: (a) "Therefore we must pay the closer attention" (2:1); (b) "Therefore...do not harden your hearts" (3:7–8); (c) "Take care, brethren" (3:12); (d) "Therefore...let us fear" (4:1)—all leading up to "Let us therefore strive" (4:11). All these statements, through the channel of 4:11, are brought to bear upon the word "for" which opens 4:12.[33]

What, then, is "the word *(logos)* of God" which brings before us "the necessity of earnest effort"? If the context is enlarged, looking now at Heb. 1:1–4:10, we see what emerges. An examination of the vocabulary of Heb. 1:1–4:13 will reveal several terms for "word" or related terms signifying forms of speaking. (1) The term *rhema*, often translated "word" or "utterance" occurs in 1:3 and 6:5 (also 11:3 and

12:9), in each case referred to as God's "Word"; (2) the term *logos* ("word") occurs in 2:2; 4:2, 12 (and in 13:7); (3) the verb *lalein* ("to speak" or "to declare") is found in 1:1, 2; 2:2, 3; 3:5; 4:8 (and 5:5; 11:18; 12:25); (4) the verb *legein* ("to say" or "to speak") occurs in 2:6, 12; 3:7, 15; 4:7 (and 5:6, 6:14; 7:21; 8:8, 9, 10, 13; 10:5, 8, 16; 12:26); (5) the verb *epein* ("to say" or "to speak") is found in 1:13; 4:3, 4 (and 10:9, 15; 13:5); (6) the verb *eipon* ("to say") occurs in 1:5; 3:10 (and 7:9; 10:7, 30; 12:21). As the texts will show, most of these examples refer to God "speaking"—a form of communication by the spoken word. The emphasis, then, is not upon "the Word of God" as "the Bible" but in terms of God's dynamic speech and creative acts.

Further, emphasis is laid upon the response of those spoken to in many of the passages (2:1–4; 3:7–11; 4:1–2, 6–8). The intention of God's "Word" was to bring about a response of faith; on many occasions, however, it was an unbelieving response or no response.

Probably, therefore, "the Word of God" (4:12) refers not to Christ ("the living Word"), for that is clear only as a Johannine usage in the New Testament (see John 1:1; 1 John 1:1; Rev. 19:13). The Word "as a sharp sword" issues from the mouth of Christ (Rev. 1:16; 19:15), so that he wields the divine Word. Further, Christ referred to his words as "spirit and life" (John 6:63) and claimed that his words would judge men on the last day (John 12:48).

Other New Testament writers—to enlarge our context further—make use of the same expression or others closely related. There is "the living and abiding word of God" (1 Pet. 1:23), identified with "the good news which was preached to you" (v. 25). Stephen referred to "living oracles" (Acts 7:38) and Paul to "the oracles of God" (Rom. 3:2). We read of "the sword of the Spirit, which is the word [*rhema*] of God" (Eph. 6:17). Luke wrote of people pressing "to hear the word of God" (Luke 5:1) from Jesus. Once again it is the divine message communicated in various forms.

Many of these expressions and speech forms will be found

in the Old Testament. In addition we read of God's speech in creation (Gen. 1:3ff.); "he sent forth his word and healed them" (Ps. 107:20); and the word from his mouth will not fail to accomplish that which he purposes (Isa. 55:11).

Returning to our passage, we see "the Word of God" characterized in five ways.[34] God's word is *living*, even as he himself (Heb. 3:12), and it is able to impart life (2 Cor. 3:6; 2 Tim. 1:10; 1 Pet. 1:23). It is also *active* (that is, full of energy; see Heb. 11:3; 1:3). It is *sharp*, beyond "any two-edged sword" (in addition to the passages cited above, see Acts 2:37 and Rev. 2:16), a symbol of conviction and judgment. It has a *piercing* quality, able to divide that which is internal and foundational to a living being, no matter how "hard or firm" it may be (Calvin). And, it has a *discerning* power, able to discover what resides in the inner being ("heart"), in that "God knows the hearts of all" (see Acts 1:24; 15:8).

This "Word of God" ultimately refers to his own Person, as the following verse (Heb. 4:13) indicates. Notice the two pronoun phrases, "before him" and "to the eyes of him," so as to say that the Word of God examines us. The passage ends with what may be a word play, as the term *logos* occurs again at the end of v. 13, reading, literally, "with whom we have a *logos*," probably meaning "a reckoning" or "an accounting." Thus God's *logos* ("word") addresses us; we then must give our *logos* ("response") to him.

Conclusion

How does a study such as we have done fit into the present day? Some will ask candidly, "Do we need to *interpret* the Bible? Why not just read it and do what it says?" Others are asking soberly, "Have our methods of interpreting the Bible proved inadequate? Ought we to declare them 'bankrupt' and get a fresh start (or return to some older methods)?"

To the former we must reply that part of "just reading" the Bible is to read it as the original readers perceived it and as we see it done in the history of Christian interpretation. Has not the same Holy Spirit worked both in the producing of the Bible and in the study of Scripture through the centuries? We see that language is not something static and unchanging but to a degree is "contingent, open, (and) ambiguous." Thus it needs to be interpreted. It can be a great help to hear "the Word of God" through the community of faith, rather than in an isolated or provincial fashion.

Some years ago I listened to a Bible lesson, an exposition of the epistle to the Philippians. The teacher did a good job communicating the basic message of the text under consideration. Several days after, I met the same teacher and remarked that I had just seen a new commentary on Philippians by a respected teacher and friend. "Have you seen it?" I asked. With rather a wry smile he replied, "No, I never read books about the Bible. I get it all on my own!" We cannot afford to be "Lone Rangers" when it comes to Bible interpretation, for truly the Bible emerged from within believing communities, and its message addressed those communities, as well as a wider readership.

To the latter group (who believe their methods have proved "bankrupt") we must reply that methods in themselves may not be good or bad. We might need to take a second look at how we have approached the Bible. Are we being self-critical regarding our methods? Are we bringing to the study of Scripture presuppositions which are running counter to its nature or its message? Have we, perhaps, relied too heavily on any one method?

Our focus is to study and interpret the Bible with reference to applying it in the life of the Church, whether corporately, in the lives of, families, or individuals. Suppose we liken it to constructing a building. Before we get on with putting up the walls or putting on a roof we need to lay a good, solid foundation (one that will give adequate support to the rest of the building). Our study and interpretation is more like laying a foundation; our application is like putting up the rest of the building.

Are we concerned about working out a biblical or a systematic theology? This is necessary to give a framework for and a substance to the proclamation of God's good news—the gospel—in today's world. To declare "the whole counsel of God" requires more than a favorite (and often isolated) Bible verse or story. Again, are we concerned about enriching the ministry of the Church by working out a pastoral theology or a theology of Christian Education? This will call for a dedicated study and expression of the nature and mission of the Church today, based upon biblical foundations.

As we have seen in the foregoing pages, interpretation is composed of many facets. There needs to be dedication to the task, reliance on the Holy Spirit, and the use of the best tools available to us. Tools for any task require at least two qualities: first, that they be good tools, suited to the work to be done and properly sharpened or tuned; second, that they be used with skill and care.

May this be an encouragement to venture into the discipline and the rewards of reading and interpreting the Bible. "Do your best to present yourself to God as one approved, a workman who has no need to be ashamed, rightly handling the word of truth" (2 Tim. 2:15).

Endnotes

INTRODUCTION

[1]H. W. Robinson, "The Higher Exegesis," *Journal of Theological Studies* 44 (1943), p. 143.

[2]R. Norris, ed., "Editorial," *Themelios* 5/2 (1980), p. 3.

[3]D. A. Hagner, "The Old Testament in the New Testament," *Interpreting the Word of God*, ed. S. J. Schultz and M. A. Inch (Moody, 1976), p. 79.

CHAPTER ONE

[1]J. A. Ernesti, *Principles of Biblical Interpretation*, trans. C. H. Terrot, (T & T Clark, 1832–33), I, p. 12.

[2]Ibid., p. 6.

[3]J. R. McQuilkin, *Understanding and Applying the Bible* (Moody, 1983), p. 63.

[4]E. D. Hirsch, *Validity in Interpretation* (Yale University Press, 1967), pp. 200–201.

[5]D. J. A. Clines, "Biblical Hermeneutics in Theory and Practice," *Christian Brethren Review* 31–32 (1982), p. 65.

[6]H. Kimmerle, "Hermeneutical Theory or Ontological Hermeneutics," trans. F. Seifert, *Journal for Theology and the Church* 4 (1967), pp. 107ff.

[7]E. Nida and C. R. Taber, *The Theory and Practice of Translation* (E. J. Brill, 1974), p. 1.

[8]Ibid., pp. 6–8.

[9]J. van Bruggen, *The Future of the Bible* (Thomas Nelson, 1978), pp. 80–84.

[10]Ibid., see discussion on pp. 99–141.

[11]Ibid., p. 79.

[12]S. H. Hendrix, "Luther Against the Background of the

History of Biblical Interpretation," *Interpretation* 37 (1983), p. 238.

CHAPTER TWO

[1]J. I. Packer, *Freedom, Authority and Scripture* (Inter-Varsity Press, 1982), pp. 16–17. It should be noted here that in contemporary theology, the "Word of God" is an expression relating not only to the Bible, but to Christ himself primarily. A secondary place was given to the Bible, and a tertiary place to the proclamation of Christ in the Church, based upon the testimony of the Bible. See J. Barr, "Scripture, Authority of," *Interpreter's Dictionary of the Bible*, Supplement, p. 795.

[2]R. Prenter, "A Lutheran Contribution," in *Biblical Authority for Today*, ed. A. Richardson and W. Schweitzer (Westminster, 1951), p. 98.

[3]R. Bultmann, "How Does God Speak to Us Through the Bible?" in *Existence and Faith*, ed. S. M. Ogden (Hodder and Stoughton, 1961), pp. 166–70.

[4]J. D. Smart, *The Interpretation of Scripture*, (SCM, 1961), p. 23.

[5]C. K. Barrett, "The Bible in the New Testament Period," in *The Church's Use of the Bible: Past and Present*, ed. D. E. Nineham (SPCK, 1963), p. 22.

[6]See J. D. Smart, *Interpretation*, pp. 204ff.; C. K. Barrett, "New Testament Period," p. 24; H. E. W. Turner, "Orthodoxy and the Church Today," *The Churchman* 86 (1972), pp. 172–73.

[7]C. F. H. Henry, *God, Revelation and Authority*, Vol. IV (Word, 1979), p. 68. He cites modern exponents of a "functional" view of biblical authority like David Kelsey (pp. 83–97), Jack Rogers (pp. 97–98), and James Barr (pp. 98–102).

[8]A. Farrer, *Interpretation and Belief*, ed. C. C. Conti (SPCK, 1976), p. 12, makes a subtle distinction, saying that in the proper sense, "verbal inspiration" means not that every word (in Scripture) is guaranteed, but that inspiration is found in the very words and nowhere else. He sees inspiration as every part of the Bible either illuminating, or receiving light from, the figure of Christ.

[9]See L. Morris, "Biblical Authority and the Concept of Inerrancy," *The Churchman* 81 (1967), pp. 22–38.

[10]G. E. Ladd, *The New Testament and Criticism* (Eerdmans, 1967), p. 12.

[11]J. Barr, review of J. K. S. Reid, *The Authority of Scripture* (Methuen, 1957), in *Scottish Journal of Theology* 11 (1958), p. 89.

[12]The article by J. Muilenburg, "Preface to Hermeneutics," *Journal of Biblical Literature* 77 (1958), pp. 18–26 is the basis for the summation of these various attempts to deal with the problem of historical relativism.

[13]See J. C. Rylaarsdam, "The Problem of Faith and History in Biblical Interpretation," *Journal of Biblical Literature* 77 (1958), pp. 26–32.

[14]G. E. Ladd, *New Testament and Criticism*, p. 27.

[15]Ibid., p. 33; R. Prenter, "Lutheran Contribution," pp. 99ff.

[16]J. Barr, "Scripture, Authority of," *IDB* Supplement, p. 797.

[17]D. Stacey, *Interpreting the Bible* (Seabury, 1979), pp. 21–23.

[18]D. Cameron, "Authority in the Church in the New Testament Period," *Churchman* 95 (1981), p. 32.

[19]R. Bultmann, *Theological Dictionary of the New Testament*, ed. by G. Kittel (Eerdmans, 1964), I. p. 697.

[20]R. S. Barbour, "The Bible—Word of God?" in *Biblical Studies: Essays in Honour of William Barclay*, ed., J. R. McKay and J. F. Miller (Collins, 1976), p. 41.

[21]J. D. Smart, *Interpretation*, p. 200.

[22]The translation here is by D. P. Fuller, "The Holy Spirit's Role in Biblical Interpretation," in *Scripture, Tradition, and Interpretation*, ed., W. W. Gasque and W. S. LaSor (Eerdmans, 1978), p. 191.

[23]H. E. W. Turner, "Orthodoxy and the Church," p. 166.

[24]R. W. Jenson, "On the Problem(s) of Scriptural Authority," *Interpretation* 31 (1977), pp. 247ff.

[25]W. Countryman, *Biblical Authority or Biblical Tyranny?* (Fortress, 1981), pp. 31ff.

CHAPTER THREE

[1]D. H. McGaughey, "The Problem of Biblical Hermeneutics," *Restoration Quarterly* 5 (1961), p. 251.

[2]C. F. H. Henry, *God, Revelation, and Authority,* III, 457.

[3]P. Helm, "Revealed Propositions and Timeless Truths," *Religious Studies* 8 (1972), pp. 127–36.

[4]D. B. Knox, "Propositional Revelation the Only Revelation," *Reformed Theological Review* 19(1960), pp. 1–9.

[5]J. Barr, *The Bible in the Modern World* (SCM, 1973), p. 123, however, cautions against equating the use of propositions in the Bible with the idea of revealed propositions or saying that revelation in general is propositional.

[6]G. Kittel (ed.), *TDNT,* IV, 137–39. See also John 10:35; Rom. 1:2; 2 Tim. 3:15–16, relating to the writings or words.

[7]J. Barr, "Revelation Through History in the Old Testament and in Modern Theology," *Interpretation* 17 (1963), p. 193.

[8]J. Barr, *Old and New in Interpretation* (SCM, 1966), p. 27.

[9]"The Chicago Statement on Biblical Hermeneutics," from the International Council on Biblical Inerrancy, Summit II, November 10–13, 1982 (italics mine); also printed in *Journal of the Evangelical Theological Society* 21(1978), pp. 289–96.

[10]G. W. Buchanan, *To the Hebrews,* Anchor Bible (Doubleday, 1972), p. 3.

[11]B. F. Westcott, *The Epistle to the Hebrews: the Greek Text with Notes and Essays* (Macmillan, 1889), p. 5. Included are many valuable references to the occurrences of the Greek words translated "in many parts and in many manners" (*polymeros* and *polytropos*) in Greek writings.

[12]E. E. Ellis, "The Authority of Scripture: Critical Judgments in Biblical Perspective," *Evangelical Quarterly* 39 (1967), pp. 196–204.

[13]E. E. Ellis, *Paul's Use of the Old Testament* (Oliver and Boyd, 1957), pp. 140–41, 146.

[14]Ellis, "The Authority of Scripture," p. 201.

[15]J. Dunn, "The Authority of Scripture According to Scripture," *Churchman* 96 (1982), p. 104.

[16]The last option—the process—is argued ably by P. Achtemeier, *The Inspiration of Scripture* (Westminster, 1980), Chap. V, pp. 105–36.

[17]E. J. Young, *Thy Word is Truth* (Eerdmans, 1957), p. 48.

[18]It is fair to say that not all inductivists would approach the problem quite this way. For a description of the methodologies involved, see P. D. Feinberg, "The Meaning of Inerrancy," in *Inerrancy,* ed. N. L. Geisler (Zondervan, 1979), pp. 269–76.

[19]J. Wenham, "Christ's View of Scripture," in *Inerrancy,* pp. 3–36.

[20]Ibid., p. 21.

[21]"The Chicago Statement on Biblical Inerrancy," p. 500.

[22]*Inerrancy,* p. 294. While this definition may appear somewhat general, Feinberg does go on, in a helpful section, to deal with observations, qualifications, and misunderstandings about inerrancy (see pp. 295–304).

[23]E. F. Harrison, "The Phenomena of Scripture," *Revelation and the Bible,* ed. C. F. H. Henry (Tyndale Press, 1959), pp. 237–50. The citations noted are taken from various parts of this essay.

[24]J. D. Smart, *Interpretation,* p. 194.

[25]L. Morris, "Biblical Authority," pp. 22–38.

[26]J. Dunn, "Authority of Scripture," p. 207. See also the essay by R. T. France, "Evangelical Disagreements About the Bible," *Churchman* 96 (1982), pp. 226–40; R. K. Johnston, *Evangelicals at an Impasse* (John Knox, 1978), pp. 15–47.

CHAPTER FOUR

[1]R. E. Murphy, "The Relationship Between the Testaments," *Catholic Biblical Quarterly* 26 (1964), pp. 350–55.

[2]Ibid., pp. 355–59.

[3]See the story of Ezra's role in rewriting the lost books by divine inspiration in 2 Esdras 14:19–48.

[4]A. Guttmann, *Rabbinic Judaism in the Making* (Wayne State University Press, 1970), p. 4.

[5]G. F. Moore, *Judaism* (Harvard University Press, 1927), I, 31–34.

[6]Ibid., p. 68.

[7]C. K. Barrett, "The Interpretation of the Old Testament in the New," in *The Cambridge History of the Bible,* ed. P. Ackroyd and C. Evans (Cambridge University Press, 1970), I, 383–384, gives the rules ascribed to Hillel:

(1) Inference from minor to major (or vice versa).
(2) Inference by analogy (two passages related by a common word or words).
(3) A family based on one member.
(4) A family based on two members.
(5) General and particular (or vice versa).
(6) Interpretation by means of a similar passage elsewhere.
(7) Inference based on the context.

[8]G. F. Moore, *Judaism*, I, p. 80.

[9]A. Guttmann, *Rabbinic Judaism*, p. 74.

[10]G. F. Moore, *Judaism*, I, p. 248.

[11]C. H. Toy, *Quotations in the New Testament* (Scribner's Sons, 1884), p. xxiii.

[12]*Babylonian Talmud*, Berakoth 4b.

[13]L. Grollenberg, *A Bible for Our Time* (SCM, 1979), p. 16, citing F. Weinreb, *The Bible as Creation* (1963).

[14]F. F. Bruce, "The Theology and Interpretation of the Old Testament," in *Tradition and Interpretation*, ed. G. W. Anderson (Oxford, 1979), p. 407; see also G. F. Moore, *Judaism*, I, p. 248: the task of the Scripture scholar is "to discover, elucidate and apply what God thus teaches and enjoins." Modern ideas of exegesis would have been foreign to Jewish and early Christian interpreters.

[15]Ibid., p. 319.

[16]Cited by C. K. Barrett, "The Old Testament in the New," pp. 384–385, from Mekhilta on Exod. 20:25 (81a).

[17]S. Jellicoe, *The Septuagint and Modern Study* (Oxford, 1968), pp. 353f.

[18]F. F. Bruce, "Interpretation of the Old Testament," pp. 408–410.

[19]See *Philo*, trans. F. H. Colson and G. H. Whitaker (W. Heinemann, 1950), II, 329ff.

[20]This is an expression found in the commentary on the book of Habakkuk, sometimes rendered "the Righteous Teacher." See T. Gaster, *The Scriptures of the Dead Sea Sect* (Secker & Warburg, 1957), esp. "Commentary on the Book of Habakkuk" (1:4; 2:1, 2).

[21]See T. Gaster, pp. 33–36.

[22]F. Josephus, *Jewish Antiquities*, trans. R. Marcus (W. Heinemann, 1958), X, 267 (Vol. VI).

[23]F. F. Bruce, "Interpretation of the Old Testament," p. 412.

[24]F. F. Bruce, *Biblical Exegesis in the Qumran Texts* (Eerdmans, 1959), pp. 9–10. For a more general study of the Qumran literature, see W. H. Brownlee, *The Meaning of the Qumran Scrolls for the Bible* (Oxford, 1964); and for some definitive and detailed examples see M. P. Horgan, *Pesharim: Qumran Interpretations of Biblical Books* (The Catholic Biblical Association of America, 1979), a revised doctoral dissertation.

[25]See the discussion in C. K. Barrett, "The Old Testament in the New," pp. 389–403.

[26]F. Buchsel, *TDNT*, I, p. 263.

[27]S. N. Gundry, "Typology as a Means of Interpretation: Past and Present," *Journal of the Evangelical Theological Society* 12 (1969), p. 234.

[28]H. W. Wolff, "The Hermeneutics of the Old Testament," in *Essays on Old Testament Interpretation*, ed. C. Westermann (SCM, 1963), pp. 180–81, 197.

[29]L. Goppelt, *Typos*, trans. D. Madvig (Eerdmans, 1982), a work originally published in German in 1939. The present edition has an extended foreward by Prof. E. Ellis.

[30]Ibid., pp. 231–32.

[31]A. T. Hanson, *Jesus Christ in the Old Testament* (SPCK, 1965), p. 7.

[32]See Melito, *Homily* 40, where *parabole* means "prefiguration" (concerning the Law).

[33]A. B. Mickelsen, *Interpreting the Bible*, pp. 236ff.

[34]M. Terry, *Biblical Hermeneutics*, pp. 250–56.

[35]P. Fairbairn, *The Typology of Scripture*, 5th ed. (T & T Clark, 1870), I, 27ff., cites the example of Cocceius who went beyond the single sense of Scripture, even, in practice, considering "a mere resemblance, however accidental and trifling" between an occurrence in the Old Testament and another in the New, to constitute the former a type of the latter.

[36]Ibid., pp. 175–205.

[37]J. D. Smart, *The Interpretation of Scripture*, pp. 129–33, stresses the "direct continuity of the Old Israel with the New" as a basis for the unity of the revelation of God's purposes. He prefers a historical-theological understanding of Scripture to a typological.

[38]D. A. Hagner, "The Old Testament in the New Testament,"

in *Interpreting the Word of God*, ed. S. A. Schultz and M. A. Inch (Moody, 1976), p. 103.

[39]D. M. Smith, Jr., "The Use of the Old Testament in the New,' in *The Use of the Old Testament in the New and Other Essays*, ed. J. M. Efird, (Duke University Press, 1972), p. 16.

[40]T. W. Manson, "The Argument from Prophecy," *The Journal of Theological Studies* 46 (1945), pp. 135–136.

[41]E. E. Ellis, "A Note on Pauline Hermeneutics," *New Testament Studies* 2 (1955–56), pp. 127ff.; see, at greater length, his *Paul's Use of the Old Testament*, (Eerdmans, 1976).

[42]D. M. Smith, Jr. "The Old Testament in the New," pp. 37–39.

[43]M. D. Hooker, "Beyond the Things That are Written?" *New Testament Studies* 27 (1981), pp. 295ff.

[44]L. Goppelt, *Typos*, p. 128.

[45]G. H. Gilbert, *Interpretation of the Bible: A Short History* (Macmillan, 1908), p. 75.

[46]F. F. Bruce, "Interpretation of the Old Testament," p. 413.

[47]C. H. Dodd, *According to the Scriptures* (Nisbet & Co., 1952), pp. 126ff.; see also F. F. Bruce, *This is That* (Eerdmans, 1968).

[48]R. N. Longenecker, *Biblical Exegesis in the Apostolic Period* (Eerdmans, 1975), pp. 205ff.

[49]E. E. Ellis, "How the New Testament Uses the Old," in *New Testament Interpretation*, p. 209ff.

[50]T. W. Manson, "The Old Testament in the Teaching of Jesus," *Bulletin of the John Rylands Library* 34 (1952), p. 332.

[51]B. S. Childs, "The Sensus Literalis of Scripture: An Ancient and Modern Problem," in *Beitrage zum Alttestamentlichen Theologie*, ed. H. Donner, et. al. (Vanderhoeck & Ruprecht, 1977), pp. 92–93.

[52]R. E. Brown, "The Sensus Plenior in the Last Ten Years," *Catholic Biblical Quarterly* 25 (1963), pp. 268–69.

[53]D. A. Hagner, "Old Testament in the New Testament," p. 92, and his excellent discussion, pp. 93–104.

[54]See R. E. Brown, "Sensus Plenior", p. 270; R. Tamisier, "The Total Sense of Scripture," *Scripture* 4 (1950), pp. 141f.

[55]R. E. Brown, "Sensus Plenior", p. 276: "In Is 7, 14, for example, if the OT does refer to a Davidic king to be born, then we

have an organic link in the Davidic birth of Christ at Bethlehem. Among the links that join Is 7, 14 and Mt 1, 23 there are the line of David, a continued and vital expectation of *the* Davidic Messiah, and the LXX rendering of the verse."

[56]J. M. Robinson, "Scripture and Theological Method: A Protestant Study in Sensus Plenior," *Catholic Biblical Quarterly* 27 (1965), pp. 23–27.

[57]M. Terry, *Biblical Hermeneutics*, pp. 384–85, rejects the idea of a "double sense' in such passages as Isa. 7:14 and Hos. 11:1. He refers to these as type and antitype, and he also distinguishes between a "double sense" and the idea that "the precious words of promise to God's people find more or less fulfillment in every individual experience" (with reference to Gen. 3:15).

[58]W. S. LaSor, "The Sensus Plenior and Biblical Fulfillment," in *Scripture, Tradition and Interpretation*, ed. W. W. Gasque and W. S. LaSor (Eerdmans, 1978), pp. 272–74.

[59]R. N. Longenecker, *Biblical Exegesis*, pp. 205ff.

[60]Ibid., p. 217.

CHAPTER FIVE

[1]P. Stuhlmacher, *Historical Criticism and Theological Interpretation of Scripture* (Fortress, 1977), p. 60.

[2]R. P. C. Hanson, "Biblical Exegesis in the Early Church," in *Cambridge History of the Bible*, I, p. 412.

[3]Ibid., p. 417.

[4]R. M. Grant, *The Bible in the Church* (Macmillan, 1958), pp. 60–61.

[5]Philo, "On the Migration of Abraham," *Loeb Classical Library* (W. Heinemann, 1932), IV, p. 253. For a recent study, see S. Sandmel, *Philo of Alexandria: An Introduction* (Oxford, 1979).

[6]R. M. Grant, *The Bible in the Church*, p. 63.

[7]Ibid., p. 65.

[8]R. P. C. Hanson, "Biblical Exegesis," p. 438.

[9]Ibid., p. 452.

[10]C. H. Kraeling, "The Jewish Community at Antioch," *Journal of Biblical Literature* 51 (1932), pp. 154–57.

[11]R. M. Grant, *The Bible in the Church*, pp. 77–81.

[12]P. Stuhlmacher, *Historical Criticism*, pp. 29–31.

[13]While Augustine laid less emphasis on an allegorical methodology in his later years, it is often for this method he is

remembered. Here is an example in his interpretation of the parable of the Good Samaritan: "The moon occurs in scripture figuratively for the mutability of human mortality. Therefore the man who fell among thieves went down from Jerusalem (which means "Vision of Peace") to Jericho, because Jericho is a Hebrew word which is interpreted in Latin as moon. He therefore, who went down as though from immortality to mortality, and fittingly was wounded by thieves and left half-dead on the road, is Adam, from whom springs the whole human race" (*Questiones Evangeliorum* 2. 19).

[14]For the Middle Ages, I have largely followed the material in R. M. Grant, *The Bible in the Church,* chap. IX.

[15]M. L. W. Laistner, "Antiochene Exegesis in Western Europe During the Middle Ages," *Harvard Theological Review* 40 (1947), p. 19.

[16]F. W. Farrar, *History of Interpretation* (Macmillan, 1886), p. 274, calls him "the Jerome of the fourteenth century."

[17]Ibid., p. 346.

[18]P. Stuhlmacher, *Historical Criticism,* pp. 32–36.

[19]R. M. Grant, *The Bible and the Church,* pp. 123–28.

[20]F. W. Farrar, *History of Interpretation,* p. 402.

[21]R. M. Grant, *The Bible and the Church,* p. 123–28.

[22]B. Ramm, *Protestant Biblical Interpretation.* Third Revised Edition (Baker, 1970), p. 63.

[23]Ibid., pp. 63–69.

[24]R. M. Grant, *The Bible and the Church,* p. 132.

[25]A major recent work examining the principles of the Enlightenment, and calling Christians to reckon with them in the study of Scripture and theology, is B. Ramm. *After Fundamentalism* (Harper & Row, 1983).

[26]For a detailed discussion and description of the role of many scholars in this period, see F. W. Farrar, *History of Interpretation,* Lecture VIII on "Modern Exegesis."

[27]A. B. Mickelsen, *Interpreting the Bible* (Eerdmans, 1963), p. 47.

CHAPTER SIX

[1]A. Wainwright, *Beyond Biblical Criticism: Encountering Jesus in Scripture* (SPCK, 1982), "Preface."

[2]See D. A. Carson, "Hermeneutics: A Brief Assessment of Some Recent Trends," *Themelios* 5/2 (1980), pp. 12–20.

[3]See his article "Hermeneutics," in *IDB*, Supplement.

[4]E. V. McKnight, *Meaning in Texts: The Historical Shaping of a Narrative Hermeneutics* (Fortress, 1978), pp. 97–99; see also *Structuralism: An Interdisciplinary Study,* ed. S. Wittig (Pickwick, 1975), pp. 2–5.

[5]G. Maier, *The End of the Historical-Critical Method* (Concordia, 1977). See the response in P. Stuhlmacher, *Historical Criticism,* pp. 66–71.

[6]D. Allister, "Truth as Existential," *Scottish Tyndale Bulletin,* (1979), pp. 8–10.

[7]G. E. Ladd, *The New Testament and Criticism,* p. 37.

[8]Ibid., p. 40.

[9]N. Cameron, "Biblical Interpretation in Some Recent Evangelical Thought," *Scottish Tyndale Bulletin* (1979), pp. 42–49; I. H. Marshall, "Biblical Interpretation in Some Recent Evangelical Thought: A Reply," ibid., pp. 50–53.

[10]D. Fuller, "Interpretation, History of," *International Standard Bible Encyclopedia,* Revised (Eerdmans, 1982), II, p. 872.

[11]See the discussion in R. de Vaux, *The Bible and the Ancient Near East* (Darton, Longman & Todd, 1972), pp. 58–62.

[12]A. L. Nations, "Historical Criticism and the Current Methodological Crisis," *Scottish Journal of Theology* 36 (1983), p. 71. This combination of historical scholarship and openness to transcendence is connected presently with the position of P. Stuhlmacher, *Historical Criticism,* p. 85: in addition to the historical method, "we must again learn to ask what claim or truth about man, his word, and transcendence we hear from these texts."

[13]J. Sandys-Wunsch, "On the Theory and Practice of Biblical Interpretation," *Journal for the Study of the Old Testament* 3 (1977), pp. 66–74.

[14]See H. Laughlin, "King David's Anger," *Psychoanalytic Quarterly* 23 (1954), pp. 87–95, where the great force of the king's answer to Nathan may be best accounted for by an unconscious guilt feeling about Bathsheba.

[15]R. Lapointe, "Hermeneutics Today," *Biblical Theology Bulletin* 2 (1972), pp. 117–18.

[16]R. Kysar, "Demythologizing the New Hermeneutic," *Journal of the American Academy of Religion* 37 (1969), p. 216.

[17]F. Lapointe, "Hermeneutics Today," p. 153.

[18]H. Kimmerle, "Hermeneutical Theory," pp. 107ff. On

the new approach, see F. Schleiermacher, *Hermeneutics: The Handwritten Manuscripts*, ed. H. Kimmerle (Scholars Press, 1977).

[19]G. Ebeling, *Introduction to a Theological Theory of Language* (Collins, 1973), p. 15.

[20]Ibid., pp. 16–17.

[21]Ibid., p. 191.

[22]Ibid., p. 209.

[23]H. Kimmerle, "Hermeneutical Theory", p. 112.

[24]H-G. Gadamer, *Truth and Method* (Sheed and Ward, 1975), p. 237.

[25]Ibid., p. 245.

[26]Ibid., p. 269.

[27]See R. Kysar, "Demythologizing," pp. 217–21.

[28]J. C. G. Greig, "Some Aspects of Hermeneutics: A Brief Survey," *Religion* 1 (1971), p. 134.

[29]C. M. Wood, *The Formation of Christian Understanding: An Essay in Theological Hermeneutics* (Westminster, 1981), pp. 24–27.

[30]A. C. Thiselton, "The New Hermeneutic," in *New Testament Interpretation*, pp. 323–29.

[31]S. M. Schneiders, "Faith, Hermeneutics, and the Literal Sense of Scripture," *Theological Studies* 39 (1978), pp. 719–36.

[32]P. D. Manson, *The Diversity of Scripture: A Theological Interpretation* (Fortress, 1982), pp. 1–12.

[33]C. F. H. Henry, *God, Revelation, and Authority*, III, p. 404.

[34]G. Turner, "Pre-understanding and New Testament Interpretation," *Scottish Journal of Theology* 28 (1975), pp. 227–42.

CHAPTER SEVEN

[1]Augustine, *On Christian Doctrine*, I.1.1.

[2]D. N. Freedman, "On Method in Biblical Studies: The Old Testament," *Interpretation* 17 (1963), p. 313.

[3]B. Ramm, *Protestant Biblical Interpretation*, pp. 128ff. For the technical study of language, Ramm adds the investigation of cognate languages and ancient translations (pp. 135f.).

[4]M. Terry, *Biblical Hermeneutics*, observes that the expression appears to have originated with K. A. G. Keil in 1788.

[5]W. C. Kaiser, Jr., *Inerrancy*, pp. 119–124.

[6]See the readable discussion in R. K. Harrison, et. al.,

Biblical Criticism: Historical, Literary and Textual (Zondervan, 1978).

[7]J. Barr, *The Semantics of Biblical Language* (Oxford, 1961), esp. pp. 107ff.

[8]K. L. Schmidt, *TDNT,* III, pp. 503–504.

[9]W. Arndt and F. W. Gingrich, *A Greek-English Lexicon of the New Testament and Other Early Christian Literature* (Chicago, 1959), p. 739.

[10]A. Thiselton, "Semantics and New Testament Interpretation," in *New Testament Interpretation,* ed. I. H. Marshall (Eerdmans, 1977), p. 79.

[11]J. Barr, "The Image of God in the Book of Genesis—A Study of Terminology," *Bulletin of John Rylands Library* 51 (1968), p. 15.

[12]The Hebrew words for "likeness" and "appearance" occur in Ezek. 1:26; "shape" in Num. 12:8 ("form" RSV); and "design" in Exod. 25:40 ("pattern" RSV).

[13]A. B. Mickelsen, *Interpreting the Bible,* p. 158.

[14]Ibid., p. 128.

[15]C. R. Taber, "Semantics," *IDB* Supplement, p. 806.

[16]See the magnificent comments on this verse in J. Denney, *The Second Epistle to the Corinthians* (Hodder and Stoughton, n.d.), pp. 193–95.

[17]E. F. Kevan, "The Principles of Interpretation," in *Revelation and the Bible,* p. 293.

[18]A. B. Mickelsen, *Interpreting the Bible,* p. 293.

[19]C. R. Taber, "Semantics," p. 802.

[20]M. Silva, *Biblical Words and Their Meaning* (Zondervan, 1983), pp. 156–57.

CHAPTER EIGHT

[1]B. Ramm, *Protestant Biblical Interpretation,* pp. 138–39 (italics his).

[2]See R. E. Brown, *The Gospel According to John XIII–XXI.* Anchor Bible (Doubleday, 1970), pp. 597–601.

[3]In this section I am heavily indebted to W. C. Kaiser, Jr., *Toward an Exegetical Theology,* pp. 91–95, 121–25 (as well as to lecture notes from his course in hermeneutics, 1971–72).

[4]W. C. Kaiser, ibid., especially chapters seven and ten.

[5]M. Terry, *Biblical Hermeneutics,* p. 90, says "nearly one

half." Only Leviticus, Ruth, Ezra, Nehemiah, Esther, Haggai and Malachi contain no poetry.

[6]The use of recent English translations from the RSV onward will help to see readily the poetic materials of the Bible, as they are printed in poetic format.

[7]See "The Method of Analogy,' in a sermon on Isa. 7:1–17 and Luke 2:1–20, E. Achtemeier, *The Old Testament and the Proclamation of the Gospel* (Westminster, 1973), pp. 165–72.

[8]D. Jodock, "Story and Scripture," *Word & World* 1 (1981), pp. 128–39.

[9]For a brief summary see H. L. Drumwright, Jr., "Wisdom," *Zondervan Encyclopedia*, V. 939–45; S. H. Blank, "Wisdom," *IDB*, IV, 852–61.

[10]H. M. Wolf, "Interpreting Wisdom Literature," *The Literature and Meaning of Scripture*, ed. M. A. Inch and C. H. Bullock (Baker, 1981), pp. 63–69.

[11]Briefly, L. Morris, *Apocalyptic* (Eerdmans, 1972); in more detail, D. S. Russell, *The Method and Message of Jewish Apocalyptic: 200 BC—AD 100* (SCM, 1964).

[12]F. C. Grant, *How to Read the Bible* (Crowell-Collier, 1961), pp. 77–78.

[13]W. C. Kaiser, Jr., *Exegetical Theology*, pp. 121–22.

[14]E. W. Bullinger, *Figures of Speech*, pp. v–xvii, has introductory comments worth reading. He affirms that "no branch of Bible study can be more important, or offer greater promise of substantial reward."

[15]Ibid., p. vi.

[16]L. Perrine, *Sound and Sense: An Introduction to Poetry* (Harcourt, Brace, 1956), pp. 52–54.

[17]E. W. Bullinger, *Figures of Speech*, pp. 755–56.

[18]The Hebrew text reads: "searching out their glory is glory." The LXX reads: "to honor noble words is fitting." Most textual scholars and commentators have suggested either emendations, or simply declared it obscure.

[19]C. H. Dodd, *The Parables of the Kingdom* (Scribner's, 1936); J. Jeremias, *The Parables of Jesus* (Scribner's, 1955). A recent, and very useful work, is R. Stein, *An Introduction to the Parables of Jesus* (Westminster, 1981).

[20]The gospel of Luke contains many parables unique to that gospel; see especially 10:25–37; 11:5–13; 12:13–22; 13:6–9;

14:7–11, 12–14; 15:8–10, 11–32; 16:1–9 (13), 19–31; 17:7–10; 18:1–8, 9–14.

[21]A. B. Mickelsen, *Interpreting the Bible*, pp. 230–31.

[22]G. B. Caird, *The Language and Imagery of the Bible* (Westminster, 1980), p. 167.

[23]Bullinger would grant this as a fable "were it not explained in verse 16," *Figures of Speech*, p. 754. But surely the application of a fable does not destroy, or change, its character.

[24]A. B. Mickelsen, *Interpreting the Bible*, pp. 204–206, includes Ezek. 17:1–24 as "an allegory and fable." The material in vv. 1–10, about the two great eagles seems to justify the point.

[25]A. B. Mickelsen, *Interpreting the Bible*, p. 200.

[26]Arndt and Gingrich, *Greek—English Lexicon*, s.v.

[27]M. Terry, *Biblical Hermeneutics*, pp. 248–50; and see A. B. Mickelsen, pp. 246–55.

[28]F. E. Gabelein, "Symbolism, Symbol," *Zondervan Encyclopedia*, V, 551.

[29]V. H. Kooy, "Symbol, Symbolism," *IDB*, IV, 472.

[30]J. R. McQuilkin, *Understanding and Applying the Bible*, p. 224.

[31]G. B. Caird, *Imagery*, p. 144.

[32]L. Perrine, *Sound and Sense*, p. 61.

[33]Ibid., pp. 88–92.

[34]G. B. Caird, *Imagery*, p. 134, n. 8.

CHAPTER NINE

[1]M. Terry, *Biblical Hermeneutics*, p. 231ff.

[2]E. Best, *From Text to Sermon: Responsible Use of the New Testament in Preaching* (John Knox, 1978), p. 8.

[3]A. E. Harvey, ed., *God Incarnate: Story and Belief* (SPCK, 1981), p. 4.

[4]E. E. Cairns, "History," *The Zondervan Pictorial Encyclopedia of the Bible* (Zondervan, 1975), III, p. 162.

[5]C. R. North, "History," *Interpreter's Dictionary of the Bible*, II, 608.

[6]R. Gordis, "Methodology in Biblical Exegesis," *JQR* 61 (1970), p. 94. He cites archaeology as "the most significant new factor in twentieth-century Biblical scholarship."

[7]C. R. North, "History," p. 608. Quotations in the following material are from this source.

[8]J. M. Meyers, *I Chronicles,* Anchor Bible (Doubleday, 1965), p. lxiii.

[9]For an excellent study of these relationships, see F. F. Bruce, *Israel and the Nations* (Eerdmans, 1969).

[10]See W. Brueggemann, *The Land* (Fortress, 1977).

[11]For a brief account, see C. F. Pfeiffer, *An Outline of Old Testament History* (Moody, 1960); at greater length, R. K. Harrison, *Old Testament Times* (Eerdmans, 1970).

[12]This is not to insist on *"the* meaning" as such. See the discussion in J. Barr, *The Bible in the Modern World,* pp. 69–73.

[13]B. Vawter, *On Genesis: A New Reading* (Macmillan, 1977), pp. 175–76.

[14](Doubleday, 1969), p. ix.

[15]The introductory data will be found also in the fuller commentaries, such as G. Milligan, *St. Paul's Epistles to the Thessalonians* (Macmillan, 1908), pp. xxi–xl; or L. Morris, *The First and Second Epistles to the Thessalonians* (Eerdmans, 1959), pp. 15ff. One of the most recent for archaeology is J. Finegan, *The Archeology of the New Testament* (Westview, 1981); see especially pp. 107–16 on Thessalonica.

[16]For example, B. Ramm, *Protestant Biblical Interpretation,* pp. 152–61, includes under the heading "cultural" a study of geography, history, and culture.

[17]Ibid., p. 152.

[18]R. de Vaux, *Ancient Israel: Its Life and Institutions* (McGraw–Hill, 1961), p. 60.

[19]J. P. Lewis, "Food," *Zondervan Encyclopedia,* II, 584.

[20]See the discussion in K. L. Schmidt, *TDNT,* I, 577–78; A. N. Sherwin-White, *Roman Society and Roman Law in the New Testament* (Oxford, 1963), pp. 24–25, says of the title "king of the Jews": "this means 'a leader of the resistance'" (citing Josephus, *Antiquities* 17.10.8).

[21]Herod Antipas, while called "king" in Mark 6:14 and 26, was in reality a "tetrarch." The term king here, something Antipas desired but never gained, appears in the popular sense.

[22]J. B. Lightfoot, *Saint Paul's Epistle to the Galatians* (Macmillan, 1896), pp. 148–49; C. F. Hogg and W. E. Vine, *The Epistle of Paul the Apostle to the Galatians* (Pickering & Inglis, 1922), pp. 163–65.

[23]A. Wikgren, "Custodian," *IDB,* I, pp. 751–52.

[24]Adapted from a discussion of New Testament studies by Alan Johnson, "History and Culture in New Testament Interpretation," in *Interpreting the Word of God*, p. 143. On the issue of cultural matters and the abiding message of Scripture, see W. C. Kaiser, Jr., "Legitimate Hermeneutics," in *Inerrancy*, pp. 141–44.

CHAPTER TEN

[1]J. D. Smart, *The Past, Present, and Future of Biblical Theology* (Westminster, 1979), p. 111.

[2]R. B. Y. Scott, "How I Interpret the Bible," *Interpretation* 5 (1951), p. 326.

[3]E. F. Kevan, "The Principles of Interpretation," p. 249.

[4]J. J. Scott, Jr., "Some Problems in Hermeneutics for Contemporary Evangelicals," *Journal of the Evangelical Theological Society* 22 (1979), pp. 74ff.

[5]N. M. de S. Cameron, *Evolution and the Authority of the Bible* (Paternoster, 1983), p. 35.

[6]M. Silva, *Biblical Words & Their Meaning*, p. 27.

[7]Ibid., pp. 25–27.

[8]C. R. North, "History," p. 609.

[9]One of the early examples was K. Stendahl, ed., *The Scrolls and the New Testament* (Scribner's, 1957).

[10]K. Leech, "Liberation Theology: The Thought of Juan Luis Segundo," *Theology* 84 (1981), p. 259. See also R. J. Sider, "An Evangelical Theology of Liberation," in *Perspectives on Evangelical Theology*, ed. K. S. Kantzer and S. N. Gundry (Baker, 1979), pp. 117–33.

[11]Tertullian, *Five Books in Reply to Marcion, Ante-Nicene Christian Library* (Vol. 18, T & T Clark, 1970), IV, 91–93; V, 283–85.

[12]See the article by J. A. Sanders, "Hermeneutics," *IDB*, Supplement, pp. 402–407, and his illustrations noted.

[13]E. Kasemann, "Thoughts on the Present Controversy about Scriptural Interpretation," in *New Testament Questions of Today* (SCM, 1969), p. 270; also P. Stuhlmacher, *Historical Criticism and Theological Interpretation of Scripture*, pp. 24–25.

[14]J. Goldingay, " 'That You May Know that Yahweh is God'; A Study in the Relationship Between Theology and Historical Truth in the Old Testament," *Tyndale Bulletin* 23 (1972), p. 64ff.

[15]I. MacPherson, "Outline of a Hermeneutical Method," *St. Mark's Review* 83 (1975), p. 12.

[16]A. J. Malherbe, "An Introduction: The Task and Method of Exegesis," *Restoration Quarterly* 5 (1961), p. 171.

[17]G. D. Fee and D. Stuart, *How to Read the Bible For All Its Worth* (Zondervan, 1981), pp. 74–75.

[18]Ibid., chapter 7.

[19]W. C. Kaiser, Jr., *Toward an Exegetical Theology*, p. 136.

[20]See G. Hasel, *Old Testament Theology: Basic Issues in the Current Debate* (Eerdmans, 1972), pp. 49–63. "It seems to be a given fact that whereas the NT is clearly *christo*centric the OT is correspondingly *theo*centric" (p. 63).

[21]P. Stuhlmacher, *Historical Criticism*, pp. 34–35.

[22]M. Dibelius and H. Conzleman, *The Pastoral Epistles* (Fortress, 1972), p. 131.

[23]B. Ramm, *Protestant Biblical Interpretation*, pp. 166–67.

[24]K. H. Rengstorf, *TDNT*, II, 140–41.

[25]Ibid., p. 146.

[26]R. B. Y. Scott, "How I Interpret", p. 324.

[27]J. D. Smart, *The Interpretation of Scripture*, pp. 55–56.

[28]I. H. Marshall, "How Do We Interpret the Bible Today?" *Themelios* 5/2 (1980), p. 9–12.

[29]A. B. Mickelsen, *Interpreting the Bible*, p. 339.

[30]Paul would hardly deny God's care for animals as such. See the precedents in Ps. 104:10ff.; Matt. 6:26.

[31]W. C. Kaiser, Jr., *Toward An Exegetical Theology*, p. 207.

CHAPTER ELEVEN

[1]D. H. Kelsey, *The Use of Scripture in Recent Theology*, pp. 197–201.

[2]J. Barr, *The Bible in the Modern World*, pp. 100–101.

[3]Adapted from R. L. Rohrbaugh, *The Biblical Interpreter* (Fortress, 1978), pp. 53–68.

[4]R. D. Culver, "Ahab," *Zondervan Pictorial Encyclopedia*, I, 78–81; H. B. MacLean, "Ahab," *IDB*, I, 61–63.

[5]J. Gray, *I & II Kings: A Commentary* (SCM, 1964), p. 389.

[6]Or, it may be an assertion, affirming Ahab's place as the supreme figure in Israel; ibid., p. 390.

[7]J. Robinson, *The First Book of Kings* (Cambridge, 1972), p. 235.

[8]See. R. L. Rohrbaugh, *The Biblical Interpreter*, pp. 62–68 for an example of interpretation that misses this point.

[9]F. Brown, S. R. Driver, C. A. Briggs, *Hebrew and English Lexicon of the Old Testament* (Oxford, 1968); see entry.

[10]For discussion of the historical background, see E. J. Young, *The Book of Isaiah* (Eerdmans, 1965), I, pp. 9–21, 266ff.; R. E. Clements, *Isaiah 1–39* (Eerdmans, 1980), pp. 78–81.

[11]J. A. Motyer, "Context and Content in the Interpretation of Isaiah 7:14," *Tyndale Bulletin* 21 (1970), p. 120f.

[12]E. J. Young, *The Book of Isaiah*, p. 279.

[13]R. E. Clements, *Isaiah 1–39*, p. 87.

[14]J. A. Motyer, "Context and Content", pp. 122–25.

[15]J. Calvin, *Commentary on the Book of the Prophet Isaiah*, trans. W. Pringle (Edinburgh, 1850), I, p. 248.

[16]The analysis is based on the essay by R. T. France, "Exegesis in Practice: Two Samples," in *New Testament Interpretation*, pp. 252–81.

[17]W. F. Albright and C. S. Mann, *Matthew*, Anchor Bible (Doubleday, 1971), p. 92.

[18]M. D. Goulder, *Midrash and Lection in Matthew* (SPCK, 1976), p. 320, prefers "son," as that is the usual meaning in Matthew. He cites 2:16; 17:18; 21:15; yet 14:2 probably means "servants."

[19]K. H. Rengstorf, *TDNT*, III, 294: The centurion's words, "I am not worthy," are here "a confession of the Messiahship of Jesus."

[20]P. A. Micklem, *St. Matthew* (Methuen, 1917), pp. 74–75.

[21]H. Schlier, *TDNT*, I, 337–38.

[22]B. Gerhardsson, "The Hermeneutic Program in Matthew 22:37–40," in *Jews, Greeks and Christians*, ed. R. Hamerton-Kelly and R. Scroggs (Brill, 1976), pp. 129–50, from which this section is adapted.

[23]R. H. Gundry, *Matthew: A Commentary on His Literary and Theological Art* (Eerdmans, 1982), pp. 448–50.

[24]B. Gerhardsson, "Hermeneutic Program," p. 134ff.

[25]J. Jeremias, *The Parables of Jesus* (SCM, 1963), p. 139ff., places it among a group of parables "with which Jesus vindicates the proclamation of the Good News to the despised and

outcast" (p. 128); and see H. F. Weiss, *TDNT,* IX, pp. 36–43, on the Pharisees.

[26]I. H. Marshall, *The Gospel of Luke: A Commentary on the Greek Text* (Eerdmans, 1978), pp. 678–79.

[27]See n. 25 for Jeremias; n. 26 for Marshall; and J. M. Creed, *The Gospel According to St. Luke: The Greek Text* (Macmillan, 1930), p. 224.

[28]For samples of other Jewish prayers in the Babylonian Talmud, see E. E. Ellis, *The Gospel of Luke* (Nelson, 1966), p. 215; S. J. Kistemaker, *The Parables of Jesus* (Baker, 1980), pp. 258–59; J. Jeremias, *The Parables,* p. 142f.

[29]J. Jeremias, ibid., pp. 192–93.

[30]W. Wink, *The Bible in Human Transformation: Toward a New Paradigm for Bible Study* (Fortress, 1973), pp. 41–43.

[31]A. Thiselton, *The Two Horizons,* pp. 14–15.

[32]B. F. Westcott, *The Epistle to the Hebrews: The Greek Texts with Notes and Essays* (Macmillan, 1889), p. 101.

[33]In the Greek text, the word *zōn* ("living") is the opening word, for sake of emphasis.

[34]See the succinct comments on these five epithets in B. F. Westcott, *Hebrews,* p. 102.

Bibliography

JOURNAL ARTICLES

Barnhart, J. E. "Every Context has a Context." *Scottish Journal of Theology* 33 (1980), pp. 501–13.

Barr, J. Review article (*The Authority of Scripture*, by J. K. S. Reid. Methuen, 1957) *Scottish Journal of Theology* 11 (1958), pp. 86–93.

———. "Biblical Hermeneutics in Ecumenical Discussion." *Student World* 60 (1967), pp. 319–24.

———. "Common Sense and Biblical Language." *Biblica* 49 (1968), pp. 377–87.

———. "The Image of God in the Book of Genesis—A Study of Terminology." *Bulletin of John Rylands Library* 51 (1968), pp. 11–26.

———. "The Old Testament and the New Crisis in Biblical Authority." *Interpretation* 25 (1971), pp. 24–40.

———. "Revelation Through History in the Old Testament and in Modern Theology." *Interpretation* 17 (1963), pp. 193–205.

Braaten, C. E. "How New is the New Hermeneutic?" *Theology Today* 22 (1965), pp. 218–35.

Brown, R. E. "The Sensus Plenior in the Last Ten Years." *Catholic Biblical Quarterly* 25 (1963), pp. 262–85.

Cameron, D. "Authority in the Church in the New Testament Period." *Churchman* 95 (1981), pp. 22–32.

Cameron, N. "Biblical Interpretation in Some Recent Evangelical Thought: The Problem of the Historical Critical Method." *Scottish Tyndale Bulletin* 30 (1979), pp. 42–49.

Carson, D. A. "Hermeneutics: A Brief Assessment of Some Recent Trends." *Themelios* 5/2 (1980), pp. 12–20.

Childs, B. S. "Jonah: A Study in Old Testament Hermeneutics." *Scottish Journal of Theology* 11 (1958), pp. 53–61.

Clines, D. J. A. "Biblical Hermeneutics in Theory and Practice." *Christian Brethren Review* 31–32 (1982), pp. 65–77.

Dunn, J. D. G. "The Authority of Scripture According to Scripture." *Churchman* 96 (1982), pp. 104–22; 96 (1982), pp. 201–25.

Ellis, E. E. "A Note on Pauline Hermeneutics." *New Testament Studies* 2 (1956), pp. 127–33.

———. "The Authority of Scripture: Critical Judgments in Biblical Perspective." *Evangelical Quarterly* 39 (1967), pp. 196–204.

Erickson, R. J. "Biblical Studies and Modern Linguistics." *Theological Students Fellowship Bulletin* 6/4 (1983), pp. 16–17.

———. "*Oida* and *Ginosko* and Verbal Aspect in Pauline Usage." *Westminster Theological Journal* 44 (1982), pp. 110–22.

Ferré, N. "Notes By a Theologian on Biblical Hermeneutics." *Journal of Biblical Literature* 78 (1959), pp. 105–14.

France, R. T. "Evangelical Disagreements About the Bible." *Churchman* 96 (1982), pp. 226–40.

Freedman, D. N. "The Interpretation of Scripture . . . the Old Testament." *Interpretation* 17 (1963), pp. 308–18.

Froehlich, K. "Biblical Hermeneutics on the Move." *Word & World* 1 (1981), pp. 140–52.

Fuller, R. C. "Trends in Biblical Interpretation." *Scripture* 4 (1952), pp. 175–80, 244–49.

Goldingay, J. "Interpreting the Bible." *Christian Brethren Review* 31–32 (1982).

———. " 'That You May Know Yahweh is God': A Study in the Relationship Between Theology and Historical Truth in the Old Testament." *Tyndale Bulletin* 23 (1972), pp. 58–93.

Gordis, R. "On Methodology in Biblical Exegesis." *Jewish Quarterly Review* 61 (1970), pp. 93–118.

Greig, J. C. G. "Some Aspects of Hermeneutics—A Brief Survey." *Religion* 1 (1971), pp. 131–51.

Grogan, G. W. "Biblical Interpretation and Theological Context." *Scottish Tyndale Bulletin* 30 (1979).

———. "The New Testament Interpretation of the Old Testament." *Tyndale Bulletin* 18 (1967), pp. 54–76.

Gundry, S. N. "Typology as a Means of Interpretation: Past and Present." *Journal of the Evangelical Theological Society* 12 (1969), pp. 233–40.

Hebert, A. G. "The Interpreter at Work." *Interpretation* 4 (1950), pp. 441–52.

Helm, P. "Revealed Propositions and Timeless Truth." *Religious Studies* 8 (1972), pp. 127–36.

Henry, C. F. H. "The Interpretation of the Scriptures." *Review and Expositor* 71 (1974), pp. 197–215.

Hirsch, E. D. "Current Issues in Interpretation." *Journal of Religion* 55 (1975), pp. 298–312.

Hooker, M. D. "Beyond the Things that are Written: St. Paul's Use of Scripture." *New Testament Studies* 27 (1981), pp. 295–309.

Jenson, R. W. "On the Problem(s) of Scriptural Authority." *Interpretation* 31 (1977), pp. 237–50.

Kaiser, W. C. Jr., "Meaning from God's Message: Matters for Interpretation." *Christianity Today* 23 (1979), pp. 30–33.

Kessler, M. "New Directions in Biblical Exegesis." *Scottish Journal of Theology* 24 (1971), pp. 317–25.

Kysar, R. "Demythologizing the New Hermeneutic Theology." *Journal of the American Academy of Religion* 37 (1969), pp. 215–23.

Lapointe, R. "Hermeneutics Today." *Biblical Theology Bulletin* 2 (1972), pp. 107–54.

Levine, B. A. "Major Directions in Contemporary Biblical Research." *Journal of Jewish Studies*, 30 (1979), pp. 179–91.

Longenecker, R. N. "Can We Reproduce the Exegesis of the New Testament." *Tyndale Bulletin* 21 (1979), pp. 3–38.

Maier, G. "Concrete Alternatives to the Historical-Critical Method." *Evangelical Review of Theology* 6 (1982), pp. 23–36.

Malherbe, A. J. "An Introduction: The Task and Method of Exegesis." *Restoration Quarterly* 5 (1961), pp. 169–78.

Manson, T. W. "The Argument from Prophecy." *Journal of Theological Studies* 46 (1945), pp. 129–36.

———. "The Old Testament in the Teaching of Jesus." *Bulletin of the John Rylands Library* 34 (1952), pp. 312–32.

McGaughey, D. H. "The Problem of Biblical Hermeneutics." *Restoration Quarterly* 5 (1961), pp. 251–56.

Marshall, I. H. "Biblical Interpretation and the Historical–Critical Method—A Reply." *Scottish Tyndale Bulletin* 30 (1979).

Marshall, I. H. "How Do We Interpret the Bible Today?" *Themelios* 5/2 (1980), pp. 4–12.

Millard, A. R., et. al. "Aspects of Biblical Interpretation." *Christian Brethren Review* 17–18 (1968), pp. 3–28, 53–54.

Morris, L. "Biblical Authority and the Concept of Inerrancy." *The Churchman* 81 (1967), pp. 22–38.

Muilenburg, J. "Problems in Biblical Hermeneutics." *Journal of Biblical Literature* 77 (1958), pp. 18–26.

Murphy, R. E. "The Relationship Between the Testaments." *Catholic Biblical Quarterly* 26 (1964), pp. 349–59.

Nations, A. L. "Historical Criticism and the Current Methodological Crisis." *Scottish Journal of Theology* 36 (1983), pp. 59–71.

Nickelsburg, G. W. E. "Reading the Hebrew Scriptures in the First Century: Christian Interpretations in Their Jewish Context." *Word & World* 3 (1983), pp. 238–50.

Nida, E. "A New Methodology in Biblical Exegesis." *Bible Translator* 3 (1952), pp. 97–111.

Osborn, R. T. "A New Hermeneutic? (Understanding and Assessing it)." *Interpretation* 20 (1966), pp. 400–411.

Packer, J. I. "Hermeneutics and Biblical Authority." *The Churchman* 81 (1967), pp. 7–21.

———. "The Reconstitution of Authority." *Crux* 18 (1982), pp. 2–12.

Payne, J. B. "Fallacy of Equating Meaning with the Human Author's Intention." *Journal of the Evangelical Theological Society* 20 (1977), pp. 243–52.

Philbin, R. J. "Some Modern Protestant Attitudes Toward Authority." *Catholic Biblical Quarterly* 21 (159), pp. 115–35.

Piper, J. "A Reply to Gerhard Maier: A Review Article." *Journal of the Evangelical Theological Society* 22 (1979), pp. 79–85.

Piper, O. A. "Principles of New Testament Interpretation." *Theology Today* 3 (1946), pp. 192–204.

Poythress, V. "Analyzing a Biblical Text: What are we after?" *Scottish Journal of Theology* 32 (1979), pp. 113–37.

Rex, H. H. "Hermeneutics Today." *Reformed Theological Review* 19 (1960), pp. 9–21.

Robinson, H. W. "The Higher Exegesis." *Journal of Theological Studies* 44 (1943), pp. 143–47.

Robinson, J. M. "Scripture and Theological Method: A Protestant Study in *Sensus Plenior,*" *Catholic Biblical Quarterly* 27 (1965), pp. 6–27.

Rowley, H. H. "The Relevance of Biblical Interpretation." *Interpretation* 1 (1947), pp. 3–19.

Rylaarsdam, J. C. "The Problem of Faith and History in Biblical Interpretation," *Journal of Biblical Literature* 77 (1958), pp. 26–32.

Sanders, J. N., "The Problem of Exegesis," *Theology* 43 (1941), pp. 324–32.

Sandys-Wunsch, J. "On the Theory and Practice of Biblical Interpretation." *Journal for the Study of the Old Testament* 3 (1977), pp. 66–74.

Schneiders, S. M. "Faith, Hermeneutics, and the Literal Sense of Scripture." *Theological Studies* 39 (1978), pp. 719–36.

Schokel, L. A. "Hermeneutics in the Light of Language and Literature." *Catholic Biblical Quarterly* 25 (1963), pp. 371–86.

Scott, J. J. Jr. "Some Problems in Hermeneutics for Contemporary Evangelicals." *Journal of the Evangelical Theological Society* 22 (1979), pp. 67–77.

Scott, R. B. Y. "How I Interpret the Bible." *Interpretation* 5 (1951).

———. "Oracles of God: The Prophetic Literature as a Medium of Revelation." *Interpretation* 2 (1948), pp. 131–42.

Senex. "Practical Scriptural Interpretation." *Scripture* 5 (1953), pp. 122–26.

Silberman, L. H. "Listening to the Text." *Journal of Biblical Literature* 102 (1983), pp. 3–26.

———. "Unriddling the Riddle: A Study in the Structure and Language of the Habakkuk Pesher (1Qp Hab.)." *Revue de Qumran* 11 (1961), pp. 323–64.

Sperber, A. "New Testament and Septuagint." *Journal of Biblical Literature* 59 (1940), pp. 193–293.

Stendahl, K. "Implications of Form Criticism and Tradition Criticism for Biblical Interpretation." *Journal of Biblical Literature* 77 (1958), pp. 33–38.

Tamisier, R. "The Total Sense of Scripture." *Scripture* 4 (1952), pp. 141–43.

Teeple, H. M. "Notes on the Theologians' Approach to the Bible." *Journal of Biblical Literature* 79 (1960), pp. 164–66.

Turner, G. "Pre-Understanding and New Testament Interpretation." *Scottish Journal of Theology* 28 (1975), pp. 227–42.

Turner, H. E. W. "Orthodoxy and the Church Today." *The Churchman* 86 (1972), pp. 166–73.

Vermes, G. "The Qumran Interpretation of Scripture in its Histori-
    cal Setting." *The Annual of Leeds University Oriental
    Society* 6 (1966–68), pp. 84–97.
Warren, P. C. "By What Authority?" *Interpretation* 1 (1947), pp.
    207–18.
Wood, C. M. "Finding the Life of a Text." *Scottish Journal of
    Theology* 31 (1978).
———. "Judgment in Interpretation." *Journal of the American
    Academy of Religion* 43 (1975), pp. 554–59.
Wood, H. G. "The Present Position of New Testament Theology:
    Retrospect and Prospect." *New Testament Studies* 4 (1958),
    pp. 169–82.
Wright, G. E. "The Christian Interpreter as a Biblical Critic."
    Interpretation 1 (1947), pp. 131–52.

BOOKS

Baillie, J. *The Idea of Revelation in Recent Thought.* Columbia
    University Press, 1956.
Barr, J. *The Bible in the Modern World.* SCM, 1973.
———. *Fundamentalism.* SCM, 1977.
———. *Old and New in Interpretation.* SCM, 1966.
———. "Scripture, Authority of." *IDB* Supplement, pp. 794–97.
Barrett, C. K. "The Bible in the New Testament Period." in *The
    Church's Use of the Bible: Past and Present.* Ed. D. E.
    Nineham. SPCK, 1963, pp. 1–24.
Bornkamm, G., G. Barth, and H. J. Held. *Tradition and Interpreta-
    tion in Matthew.* Trans. P. Scott. SCM, 1963.
Bruce, F. F. *Biblical Exegesis in the Qumran Texts.* Eerdmans, 1959.
———. "The Theology and Interpretation of the Old Testament."
    in *Tradition and Interpretation.* Ed. G. W. Anderson.
    Oxford University Press, 1979, pp. 385–416.
———. *This is That: The New Testament Development of Some
    Old Testament Themes.* Eerdmans, 1968.
Bultmann, R. "How Does God Speak to Us Through the Bible?"
    in *Existence and Faith.* Ed. S. M. Ogden. Hodder and
    Stoughton, 1961, pp. 166–70.
———. "Is Exegesis Without Presuppositions Possible?" in *Existence
    and Faith,* pp. 289–96.
Cameron, N. M. de S., *Evolution and the Authority of the Bible.*
    Paternoster, 1983.

Childs, B. S. "The Sensus Literalis of Scripture: An Ancient and Modern Problem," in *Beitrage zur Alttestamentlichen Theologie.* Ed. H. Donner, *et. al.* Vandenhoeck & Ruprecht, 1977, pp. 80–93.

Countryman, W. *Biblical Authority or Biblical Tyranny?* Fortress, 1978.

Danker, F. W. *Multipurpose Tools for Bible Study.* Second Edition. Concordia, 1966.

Dodd, C. H. *According to the Scriptures.* Nisbet & Co., 1952.

Ebeling, G. *Introduction to a Theological Theory of Language.* Collins, 1973.

Efird, J. M. *How to Interpret the Bible.* John Knox, 1984.

Ellis, E. E. "How the New Testament Uses the Old," in *New Testament Interpretation.* Ed. I. H. Marshall. Eerdmans, 1977, pp. 199–219.

Ernesti, J. A. *Elementary Principles of Interpretation.* Trans. M. Stuart. Gould and Newman, 1838.

Evans, C. F. "Hermeneutics," in *Explorations in Theology 2.* SCM, 1977.

Farrer, A. *Interpretation and Belief.* Ed. C. C. Conti. SPCK, 1976.

Fee, G. D. and D. Stuart. *How to Read the Bible For All Its Worth.* Zondervan, 1981.

France, R. T. "Exegesis in Practice: Two Samples," in *New Testament Interpretation.* Ed. I. H. Marshall. Eerdmans, 1977, pp. 252–81.

Fuller, D. L. "The Holy Spirit's Role in Biblical Interpretation," in *Scripture, Tradition, and Interpretation.* Ed. W. W. Gasque and W. S. LaSor. Eerdmans, 1978, pp. 189–98.

———. "Interpretation, History of," *International Standard Bible Encyclopedia.* Ed. G. W. Bromiley. Eerdmans, 1982, II, 863–74.

Gadamer, H-G. *Truth and Method.* Sheed & Ward, 1975.

Gerhardsson, B. "The Hermeneutic Program in Matthew 22:37–40," in *Jews, Greeks and Christians.* Ed. R. Hamerton-Kelly and R. Scroggs. Brill, 1976, pp. 129–50.

Gilbert, G. H. *Interpretation of the Bible: A Short History.* Macmillan, 1908.

Goppelt, L., *Typos.* Trans. D. Madvig. Eerdmans, 1982.

Grollenberg, L. *A Bible for Our Time.* SCM, 1979.

Gruenler, R. C. *New Approaches to Jesus and the Gospels: A*

Phenomenological and Exegetical Study of Synoptic Christology. Baker, 1982.

Guttman, A. *Rabbinic Judaism in the Making.* Wayne State University Press, 1970.

Hagner, D. "The Old Testament in the New Testament," in *Interpreting the Word of God.* Ed. S. J. Schultz and M. A. Inch. Moody, 1976, pp. 78–104.

Hanson, A. T. *Jesus Christ in the Old Testament.* SPCK, 1965.

Hanson, P. D. *The Diversity of Scripture: A Theological Interpretation.* Fortress, 1982.

Harrison, E. F. "The Phenomena of Scripture," in *Revelation and the Bible.* Ed. C. F. H. Henry. Tyndale Press, 1959, pp. 237–50.

Hasel, G. *Old Testament Theology: Basic Issues in the Current Debate.* Revised Edition. Eerdmans, 1975.

———. *New Testament Theology: Basic Issues in the Current Debate.* Eerdmans, 1978.

Henry, C. F. H. *God, Revelation and Authority.* Vol. III–IV Word, 1979.

Kelsey, D. *The Uses of Scripture in Recent Theology.* Fortress, 1975.

Kevan, E. F. "The Principles of Interpretation," in *Revelation and the Bible.* Ed. C. F. H. Henry. Tyndale Press, 1959, pp. 285–98.

Ladd. G. E. *The New Testament and Criticism.* Eerdmans, 1967.

LaSor, W. S. "The *Sensus Plenior* and Biblical Interpretation," in *Scripture, Tradition, and Interpretation.* Ed. W. W. Gasque and W. S. LaSor. Eerdmans, 1978, pp. 260–77.

Liefeld, W. L. *New Testament Exposition: From Text to Sermon.* Zondervan, 1984.

Longenecker, R. *Biblical Exegesis in the Apostolic Period.* Eerdmans, 1975.

Martin, G. *Reading Scripture as the Word of God: Practical Approaches and Attitudes.* Servant Books, 1982.

Martin, R. P. "Approaches to New Testament Exegesis," in *New Testament Interpretation.* Ed. I. H. Marshall. Eerdmans, 1977, pp. 220–51.

McQuilkin, J. R. *Understanding and Applying the Bible.* Moody, 1983.

Moore, G. F. *Judaism.* Harvard University Press, 1927.

Nicole, R. "New Testament Use of the Old Testament," in *Revelation and the Bible*. Ed. C. F. H. Henry. Tyndale Press, 1959, pp. 237–50.

Nida, E. A. and C. R. Taber. *The Theory and Practice of Translation*. Brill, 1974.

Nixon, R. "The Authority of the New Testament," in *New Testament Interpretation*. Ed. I. H. Marshall. Eerdmans, 1977, pp. 334–50.

Packer, J. I. *Freedom, Authority & Scripture*. IVP, 1982.

Richardson, A. and W. Schweitzer (ed.). *Biblical Authority for Today*. Westminster, 1951.

Rohrbaugh, R. L. *The Biblical Interpreter*. Fortress, 1978.

Rowley, H. H. "The Authority of the Bible," in *From Moses to Qumran*. Lutterworth, 1963, pp. 3–31.

de Saussure, F. *Course in General Linguistics*. Trans. W. Baskin. Fontana, 1974.

Schleiermacher, F. *Hermeneutics*. Ed. H. Kimmerle. Scholars Press, 1977.

Shires, H. M. *Finding the Old Testament in the New*. Westminster, 1974.

Silva, M. *Biblical Words & Their Meaning: An Introduction to Biblical Semantics*. Zondervan, 1983.

Smart, J. D. *The Interpretation of Scripture*. SCM, 1961.

Smith, D. M., Jr. *The Use of the Old Testament in the New and Other Essays*. Ed. J. M. Efrid. Duke University Press, 1972.

Stonehouse, N. B. "Special Revelation as Scriptural," in *Revelation and the Bible*. Ed. C. F. H. Henry. Tyndale Press, 1959, pp. 75–86.

Tasker, R. V. G. *The Old Testament in the New Testament*. Eerdmans, 1963.

Thiselton, A. C. "The New Hermeneutic," in *New Testament Interpretation*. Ed. I. H. Marshall. Eerdmans, 1977, pp. 308–33.

———. "Semantics and New Testament Interpretation," in *New Testament Interpretation*, pp. 75–104.

Toy, C. H. *Quotations in the New Testament*. Scribner's Sons, 1884.

Wells, P. R. *James Barr & the Bible: Critique of a New Liberalism*. Presbyterian and Reformed, 1980.

Wilder, A. N. "New Testament Hermeneutics Today," in *Current Issues in New Testament Interpretation*. Ed. W. Klassen and G. F. Snyder. SCM, 1962, pp. 38–52.

Wolff, H. W. "The Hermeneutics of the Old Testament," in *Essays on Old Testament Interpretation*. Ed. C. Westermann. SCM, 1963, pp. 160–99.

Wood, C. M. *The Formation of Christian Understanding*. Westminster, 1981.

Young, E. J. *Thy Word is Truth*. Eerdmans, 1957.